POMPEII

UNDER THE VOLCANO

GUIDE TO THE TOWN BURIED BY MOUNT VESUVIUS 2000 YEARS AGO

GUIDE TURISTICHE FORTUNA AUGUSTA

POMPEI 1999

On a summer morning in 79 AD, Pompeii was buried after an unexpected and dramatic eruption of the volcano Mount Vesuvius. The tragedy left little possibility of survival for the estimated 10,000 people who lived in the town.

POMPEII
UNDER THE VOLCANO

CONTENTS

POMPEII
UNDER THE VOLCANO

CONTENTS

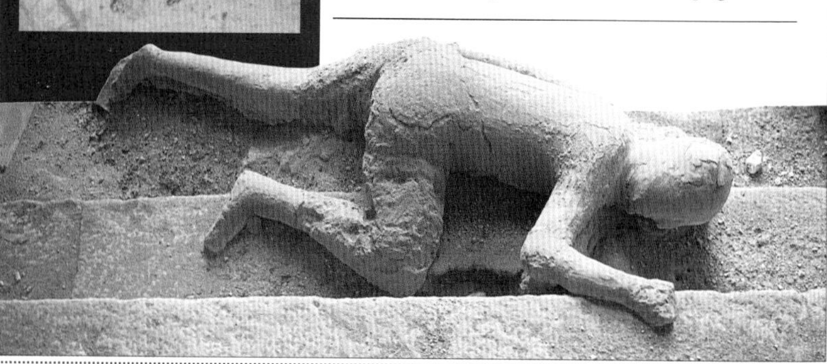

POMPEII- THE TOWN ON THE SEA

Pompeii and the sea, at the centre of the Gulf of Naples, a fact that could be the key to understanding the birth of the city. The navigability of the nearby River Sarno, the intersection of main roads and the ease with which it was possible to land from the sea, made its fortune.

The first settlement was established by the Etruscans at the end of the 7th century BC, on a pre-existing Oscan settlement (the Oscans being the Italic people who lived in the region); the first city wall, with an area of approximately 63 hectares, representing nearly the whole surface area occupied by the present-day town, was built in this period.

In this first phase the city saw a period of sparse residential development, with small groups of houses built at roadsides and large areas designated for vegetable and ornamental gardens.

The Etruscans, coming from central Italy, established themselves in many parts of the region and Pompeii provided an ideal location for a settlement in terms of trade as it had a safe harbour. Urban development, however, was in contrast with the hegemony of Greek settlers, who had lived on the nearby island of Ischia since 770 B.C., and later in the town of Cumae and on other parts of the coast, such as Neapolis. Etruscan influence lasted until the Battle of Cumae in 524 B.C. when they were defeated at the hands of the Greeks, marking

The Triangular Forum was a type of acropolis.

CHRONOLOGICAL TABLE:

The Oscans found the first settlement. 7th century B.C.	The Greeks defeat the Etruscans in the sea battle at Cumae. 524 B.C.	Rome is victorious over the Samnites and assumes control of the Campania 343 - 290 B.C.
6th century B.C. Etruscan influence and growth of the town.	423 B.C. The Samnites conquer Capua, then Cumae, and later the whole Campania region.	218 - 203 B.C. Hannibal invades Italy.

the end of Etruscan influence. Towards the end of the 5th century B.C. the Samnites, a people from the mountains, conquered the region today known as Campania, and replacing the Greeks and the Etruscans, assumed control of the area, taking possession of Pompeii too.

The influence of the Greeks, more cultured and developed, lasted in spite of harsh Samnite rule.

During this phase the town continued to develop and the defensive wall was reinforced with an "orthostatic" curtain, so called because of its skirting of vertical blocks. The long Samnite wars between 343 and 290 B.C. ended in victory for Rome and in a period of growth for Pompeii. Pompeii kept its free status and became a confederate town, entering the Roman-Italic economy. Under these conditions the Samnite Pompeii began a period of prosperity and increase in trade based mainly on wine and oil export. Financial well-being led to much rebuilding for both practical and ornamental purposes. In the 2nd century B.C. all public buildings were redeveloped and embellished - the Etruscan Temple of Apollo, the Basilica and the Temple of Jupiter, for example.

A two-storey colonnade was built along three sides of the Forum which became the centre of reli-

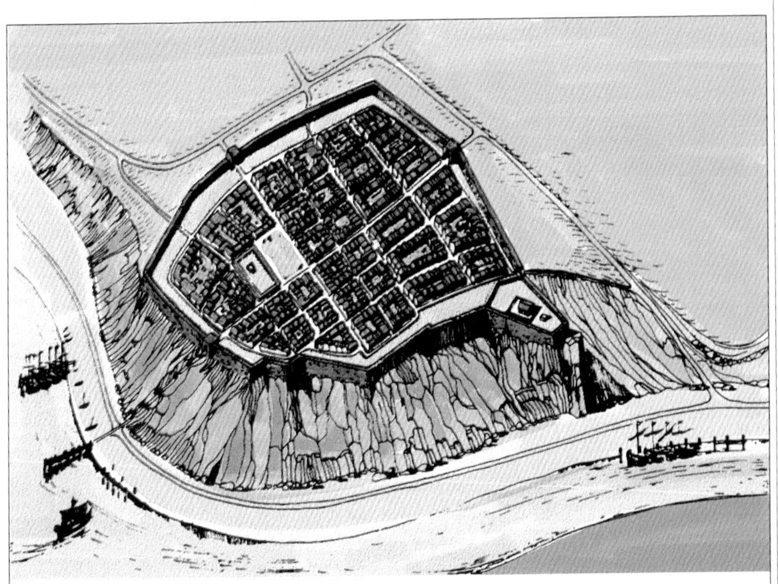

Pompeii stands on a mound which rises some 30 metres above sea level, the result of a lava flow from Mount Vesuvius in an earlier period. Being completely without water, it was difficult to live there, but its dominant position looking over both the plain behind and the bay in front meant that it was easy to see any potential aggressors arriving from any direction, as well as making it relatively easy to defend.

The first inhabited centre, the *Altstadt*, has been identified as being the areas around the Forum, in the zone included in the VIII Regio, between the vicolo dei Soprastanti, via degli Augustali, via del Lupanare and the via dei Teatri.

This would have been a small group of buildings constructed according to the geographical features of the land, rather than having a proper urban plan.

Pompeii becomes an ally of Rome. 2nd century B.C..	Octavius takes power and becomes Augustus Caesar, the first Roman emperor. 27 B.C.	Pompeii is seriously damaged by an earthquake (grade 6 on the Richter 62 A.D.
80 B.C. Revolt of the Italic towns against Rome. Pompeii is defeated and proclaimed a Roman colony.	59 A.D. Fight in the Amphitheatre between the inhabitants of Pompeii and those of Nuceria.	79 A.D. Eruption of Vesuvius and total destruction of the town.

gious, political and administrative life.
During the social war Pompeii allied itself with other Italic settlements against Rome to fight for Roman citizenship.
Silla, the Roman Consul, arrived in Campania in 89 B.C. in order to quell the revolt in the Italic towns and on the 30th of April of that year sacked and took possession of Stabiae.
Herculaneum fell at the beginning of June. In the meantime Pompeii had reinforced its walls, building some towers on the north side. Considering it useless to try and resist to the bitter end, the town eventually surrendered.
The Romans invaded the town and proclaimed it a colony calling it *Colonia Cornelia Venerea Pompeianorum* after Lucius Cornelius Silla and the Goddess Venus (of whom Silla was a devout follower).
The town then underwent a new period of transformation. First, many of the soldiers who had fought in Silla's army were awarded plots of land.

The Basilica.

Pompeii lost its status as a free Italic town and obtained a Roman legal co-de and constitution.
Consequently, for a lengthy period, positions of power in local government were occupied by the newly-arrived, and no longer by representatives of the principal local families, such as the Popidius, the Trebius and the Holconius families.
This in turn gave the city a clear sign of "Romanisation"; so the Samnite Temple of Jupiter was dedicated to the Capitoline triad of Jupiter, Juno and Minerva and transformed into the Capitolium.
The temple of Venus was also built at this time on the spur of the hill overlooking the sea. The Forum Baths were built behind the Capitolium following the Roman style. The Odeion was built in the nearby theatre to provide a venue for musical and literary recitals, and an Amphitheatre was erected against the wall in the southern part of the town.
With the rise to power of Augustus Caesar and the proclamation of the Empire, Pompeii moved into a new period of transformation. From 20 B.C. onwards the symbols of the Empire had a notable impact on Pompeii. The temples of Augustus' favourite deities were embellished and the worship

Imaginary reconstruction of the Forum colonnade.

of these deities became synonymous with worshipping the Emperor.
The Temple of Venus was rebuilt in marble and extended while the cult of the Emperor was further consolidated by the building of the Temple of Vespasian in the Forum. The temple was built of marble and, according to an inscription, dedicated to the genius of Augustus.
The Building of Eumachia, seat of the corporation of wool-workers, was dedicated to the Concordia and to the Pietas Augusta. The Forum square was also modified and cleared of the statues of the honoured Pompeiians, and foundations were laid for monumental equestrian statues and three quadrigae dedicated to the emperors.
Various honorary arches were built which served as "privileged podiums" for imperial statues. The large arch, known as the Arch of Nero, on the eastern side of the Capitolium is one such example.
The temples of the imperial cult were also built outside the Forum area, for example the Temple of Fortuna Augusta.

THE DEATH OF POMPEII

THE PREMONITORY EARTHQUAKE

The eruption that buried Pompeii was preceded by a period of intense seismic activity. *"For many days before there had been various tremors, which had not been taken into account, because of their frequency in Campania"* writes Pliny the Younger in his second letter to Tacitus.

In 62 A.D., seventeen years before Pompeii was buried, a violent earthquake (grade 6 on the Richter scale) seriously shook the town with a large number of people killed and considerable damage done to buildings.

Thanks to its flourishing economy and to contributions of patrons with political ambitions, Pompeii quickly began to repair the damage that the areas of public interest had suffered.

The reconstruction work also included the houses, some of which were not only repaired, but extended and refurbished.

When the final catastrophe came, some of the reconstruction work was still in progress, as can be seen from the remains of building sites still open in various parts of the town.

THE ERUPTION OF 79 A.D.

"A cloud formed..., the only way I can describe it is to say that its appearance and shape were similar to that of a cluster pine tree". This is the apocalyptic image of Vesuvius that met the eyes of the terrified inhabitants on the morning of Pompeii's final day, the 24th of August 79 A.D. Up until then the volcano had been

Many raised their arms to implore the gods, others said that there were gods no more, and that this was the last night of the world. From Pliny's second letter to Tacitus.

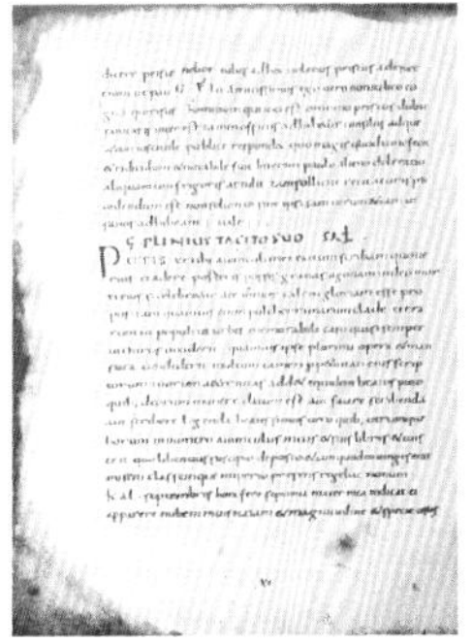

Letter from Pliny the Younger to Tacitus.

thought of merely as a mountain.
We owe this description to Pliny the Younger, admiral of the Roman fleet stationed at Miseno and an expert naturalist who, in two letters to Tacitus, tells of the death of his uncle, Pliny the Elder. Pliny the Younger left Miseno with a few ships and headed for Stabiae to his friend Pomponianus.
"Continuous and prolonged tremors shook the house," he wrote in his first letter to Tacitus. *"It was almost as if it were being pulled up from its foundations, one moment it seemed lower, the next higher. However, people were afraid of the shower of lapilli stones falling outside, however light and porous they might be; ... he chose to go outside ... he put some pillows on his head and secured them with sheets."* The catastrophe probably began towards twelve o'clock of the 24th of August with a deafening noise. The "plug" of solidified lava that had formerly sealed the volcano's summit was ripped apart by the huge build up of pressure below. The explosion projected a 20 km high co-

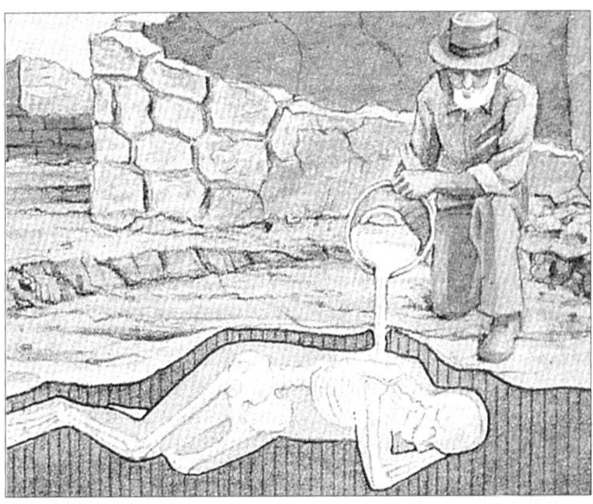

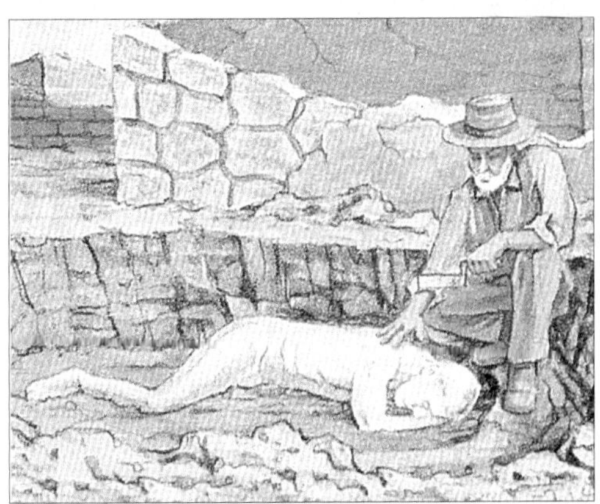

We can see some of the tragic death scenes in the plaster casts made by archaeologists using Giuseppe Fiorelli's technique.
The archaeologist poured liquid plaster into the hollows left in the ash when the bodies had decomposed to recreate the figures at the moment of their death.
This technique can be used for any material that decomposes, particularly wood, and has allowed plaster casts to be made of doors, windows, stairs and other parts of the houses in Pompeii.

lumn of volcanic materials into the air, and this was followed by a shower of small "lapilli" (pumice stones) and then of volcanic ash, which settled over a 70 kilometres radius to the south east.
Pompeii in a surreal twilight of a morning suddenly darkened, and was buried in the course of a few hours.
Volcanic material fell, there were earth tremors and tidal waves, the morning of the day after. At the end of the eruption the rain carried away downhill the large amount of materials settled on the sides of the volcano, disguised as impressive rivers of mud.
Herculaneum was covered by 20 metres of solidified mud, probably produced also by the ground water table that flew into the magma chamber of the volcano.
Most of the inhabitants of Pompeii were killed not by the collapsing buildings or the volcanic shower of stones and ash, but by the poisonous gases released from the pumice stones.

Pompeii was submerged under 4 metres of ash and lapillus.

THE DAY AFTER

When the fury stopped, the sun illuminated a landscape that seemed lunar.
The land all the way from Naples to Stabiae was covered in a blanket of dark ash.
There were no longer any houses, roads or trees. All forms of life had been wiped out.
A few days after the eruption an imperial commission of senators arrived from Romc to access the damage and organise aid for the people.
The commission asked the Emperor Titus to help in repairing the damage to the town. In 80 A.D. the Emperor came in person to the disaster areas but decided not to undertake any work in favour of the irredeemably buried towns of Pompeii and Herculaneum. The inhabitants who had survived the disaster attempted to recover statues of their Gods and sacred objects; others looked for the bodies of their dear ones.
The site of Pompeii remained barren and the inhabitants looked elsewhere for refuge, abandoning the now-inhospitable place for ever.
The emperor Alexander Severus (208-235 A.D.) began excavations to recover marble, columns and statues, but the works were soon interrupted.
From then on Pompeii was completely forgotten.
All that was left of the towns were vague directions on Roman maps, such as the Tabula Peutingeriana, which were reproduced up to the Middle Ages.

The House of Fabius Rufus. Plaster casts.

THE DISCOVERY OF POMPEII

In 1592, while digging a canal in the area known as "collina della Civita", **the architect Fontana** found ruins of buildings with decorated walls. The find was documented and left at that, and the work on the canal continued. Excavations in that area, began in 1748 during the reign of Charles of Bourbon. They erroneously believed to be searching for the ancient Stabiae, at only 200 metres from the Temple of Fortuna Augusta.

In 1763 the discovery of an inscription enabled it to be certified that the town brought to light was in fact Pompeii. Excavation work made better progress in Pompeii than in Herculaneum, which was covered by a mud slide, as it was much harder to remove the hardened blanket of solidified mud than it was to dig out Pompeii from the layers of ash and lapilli stones.

The sensational discoveries made a deep impression on contemporary observers, and in the 17th century Pompeii became an essential stop on the *Grand Tour of Italy*. Excavations became more scientifically rigorous in 1860 when **Giuseppe Fiorelli** was appointed director of the archaeological site at Pompeii. It was Fiorelli who first introduced a methodology which combined discovery with the concept of conservation. Excavations became rational, well-planned and co-ordinated with an overall strategy, instead of the haphazard search for precious objects and important buildings that it had previously been.

Pompeii is also associated with **Amedeo Maiuri** who was responsible for the discovery of many items between 1924 and 1961 and who was the author of fundamental studies.

It is thanks to him that many important chapters have been written in the great book of archaeology that we call Pompeii. **Giuseppe Spano**, a figure from the

Excavation work in progress in the Temple of Isis.

academic world who worked as the director of the archaeological digs during Maiuri's directorship, was the author of many works that have helped in understanding the history of the settlements around Mount Vesuvius.

The contemporary period has been characterised not only by new discoveries, but also by serious problems regarding the preservation of what was found in the past and by the need to open up new chapters in the history of Pompeii as part of an interdisciplinary approach.

Imaginary reconstruction of one of the shops on Via di Mercurio.

Mount Vesuvius

Bacchus and MountVesuvius from the House of the Centenary

Mount Vesuvius is known as a "composite volcano" in that it is the result of the accumulation of materials thrown up by preceding eruptions. This material, as well as "constructing" the volcano, continuously modifies its physiognomy with sequences of explosions which can even build up enough force to destroy entire parts of the mountain.
Vesuvius erupted eleven times in the following 12 centuries, of which the most violent occurred in 1139.The eruptions then became less frequent and in the 14th century there was a long period of inactivity. During this time the volcano was covered in lush vegetation.
In the late 16th century there were various tremors which were almost a forewarning of the catastrophic eruption that was to take place on 16 December 1631. This eruption was almost equal in violence to that of 79 A.D., and caused the deaths of approximately 4,000 people.
Other violent eruptions followed, such as the one in 1707 when the Austrian garrison was stationed in Naples, and that of 1794 which destroyed Torre del Greco. There were other major eruptions in 1895 and 1899 and successivamente in 1906 and 1944.
1845 saw the setting up of the Mount Vesuvius Observatory near the crater at Herculaneum. It is a scientific station which keeps a constantly vigilant eye on the volcano's activity. This can be seen from the wisps of smoke inside the crater and from a moderate amount of seismic activity.

View of Vesuvius and the Gulf of Naples fom Mount Faito.

During the MiddleAges, MountVesuvius was considered the mouth of hell .

The history of the eruptions of Mount Vesuvius is complex: there have been Plinian eruptions, such as the one that destroyed Pompeii, par oxysmic eruptions such as that of 1944, Hawaiian eruptions with a fountain of lava, as in 1779, Etnaean with off-centred conic formations, as in 1760, 1794 and 1861. Finally, the activity inside the crater behaves in the manner of the Stromboli volcano. Experts have estimated that some three kilometres of lava came forth from the volcano in 79 B.C., coming out at a speed of 400,000 metres per second. Eruptions this powerful and destructive are called Plinian after the Roman naturalist Pliny. Before 79 B.C. there were five eruptions of this type: 25,000, 19,000, 15,000, 7,900 and 3,700 years ago.

1 THE IMPERIAL VILLA

The villa, built during the first imperial age, is laid out on the natural slope of the hill on which the town of Pompei was founded. The villa was destroyed by the earthquake of 62 A.D. and was never rebuilt although the 80-metre-long colonnade with its 43 columns is still visible today. They were originally decorated with white stucco to create a fluted effect, framed inside niches. The walls of the living room depict the legend of Theseus slaying the Minotaur, Theseus abandoning Ariadne, the flight of Daedalus and the fall of Icarus.

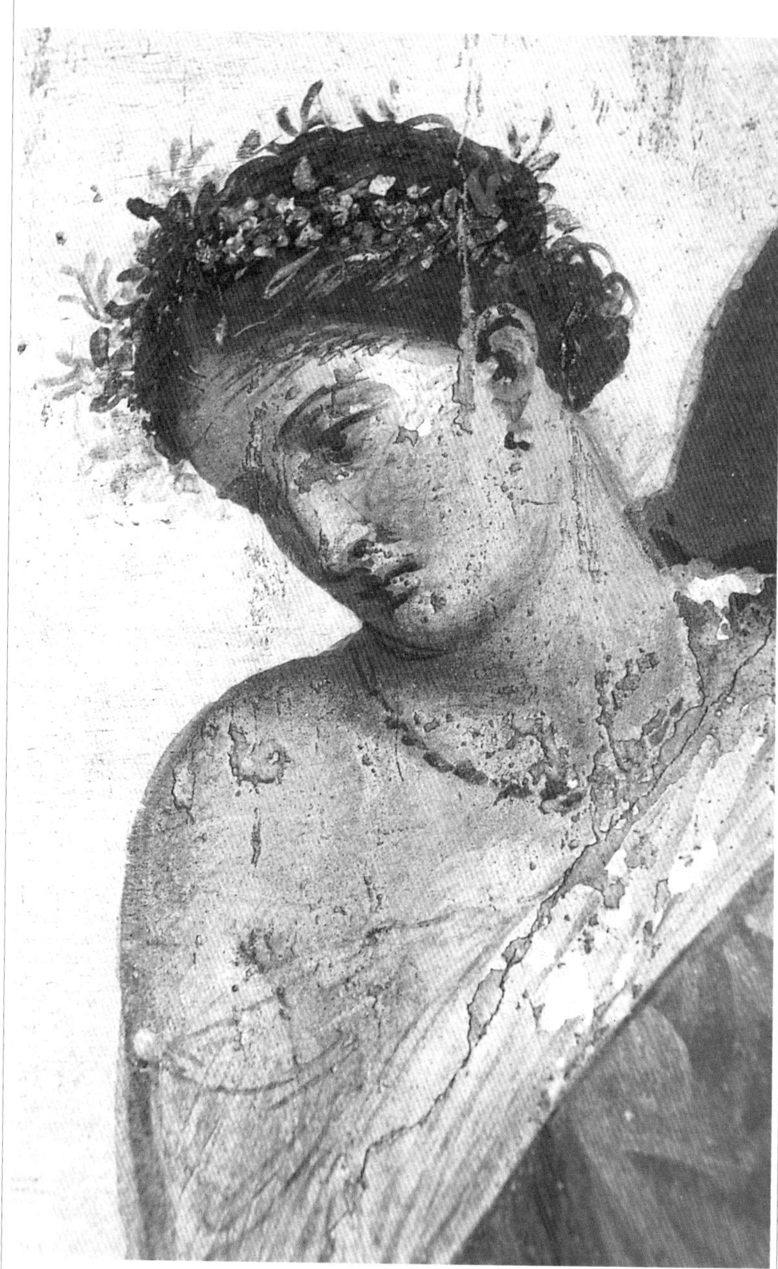

The flight of Daedalus and the fall of Icarus. Detail of the nymph.

2 THE SUBURBAN BATHS

The baths complex, not actually very big, stood just outside the town walls, and was probably used by people coming from outside the town. The walls of the changing room were decorated with eight fresco paintings of a highly erotic nature. This initially led to the conclusion that this area must have been a *lupanar* (brothel) annexed to the baths. It has however been otherwise suggested that in this case, the erotic frescoes were probably a humorous method of reminding customers where they had left their clothes by assigning a number and an amusing painting to each of the various chambers.

3 THE PORTA MARINA GATE

Once the gateway into the town from the harbour, it is now the main entrance into the archaeological site. The gate itself is incorporated into a tower with two arched passageways: one was served by stairs

for pedestrians while the other was both wider and higher and was used by carts and wagons.

The Porta Marina.
The gate linked the town to the harbour on the coast.

4 THE TEMPLE OF VENUS

This was the temple of the goddess to whom Silla dedicated the colony in calling it *Cornelia Veneria Pompeianorum*. The building, made entirely of marble, was situated in the part of the town with the best view out to sea. Little of the temple now remains as a result of the damage it suffered in the earthquake of 62 A.D. and also because it was stripped of its marble after the eruption of 79 A.D..

Imaginary reconstruction of the Temple of Venus.

5 THE TEMPLE OF APOLLO

The temple dedicated to the god Apollo had probably been present in Pompeii ever since the town was founded. Interest in the cult of Apollo began to dwindle in Pompeii in the 5th century BC but the ancient temple survived for a further 3 centuries before being replaced by a new structure. The temple was surrounded by Corinthian columns with a travertine stone altar at the foot of the long flight of stairs and a sun dial slightly to one side. To the right of the long side of the portico we find the bronze statue of Apollo with a bow and arrow opposite a bust of Diana. Alongside the columns marking the entrance to the temple stood two statues: Venus and a small altar on one side and a Hermaphrodite on the other.

Portico of the Temple of Apollo.

View of the Temple of Apollo.

Imaginary Reconstruction of the temple.

6 THE BASILICA

This majestic building housed the town's law courts from the 2nd century B.C. and, according to an engraving found during archaeological digs, was called the "bassilica". Its position close to the Forum made certain that it was frequently visited. Evidence of this can be seen in the hundreds of examples of graffiti, including some particularly vulgar expressions, scratched onto the walls.

The 28 wide brick columns, each 11 metres in height, surrounded the spacious central area. At the end of this area there is a small dais, raised about two metres from the ground, which seems to be an altar but is in fact the seat of the judge. The lack of a permanent staircase can be explained by the need to guarantee the judge's isolation and safety from the frequently violent reactions of the citizens standing trial. Hence a wooden staircase was probably provided.

Detail of the double order of columns in the Tribunal.

Aerial view. The large covered areas of the Basilica were a favourite meeting-place for the townspeople.

It is quite likely that this was also a place where businessmen would make deals, a sort of "stock market" in the centre of a town in which commercial trading played a crucial role in the local economy.

PLAN OF THE CIVIC FORUM

1 Temple of Apollo
2 Basilica
3 Civic Forum
4 Municipal Buildings
5 Comitium
6 Building of Eumachia
7 Temple of Vespasian
8 Temple of the Public Lares
9 Macellum
10 Arch of Nero
11 Capitolium
12 Arch of Drusus
13 Public Toilet
14 Grain Stores (Horrea)
15 Mensa Ponderaria
16 Suggestum

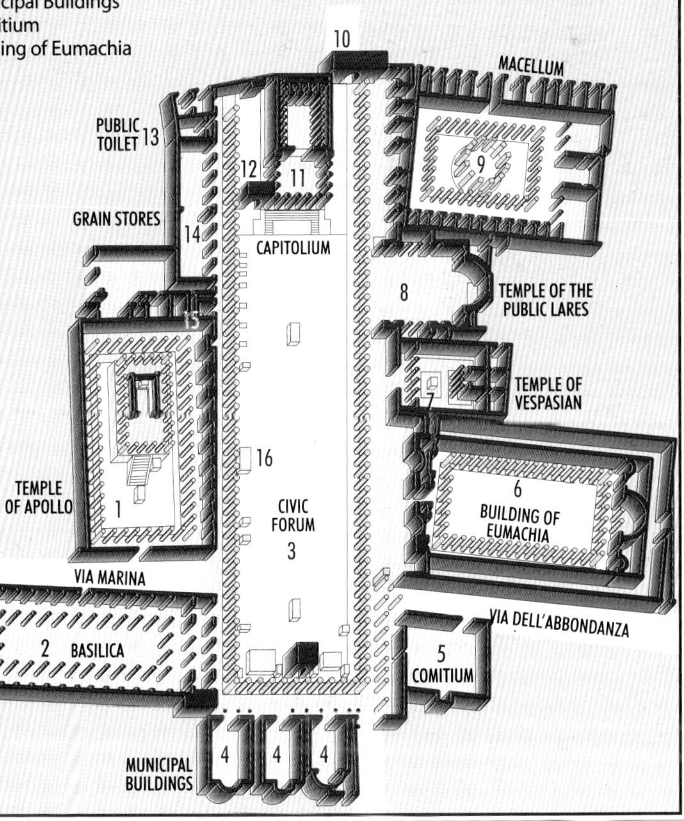

Imaginary reconstruction of the Forum.

DINONV· NIREFALOMI·

HALCIDICVMC

7 THE FORUM

The Forum was the main square in Pompeii and was reserved exclusively for pedestrians. This was the very heart of Pompeii's daily life and housed the most important municipal, religious and commercial buildings in the town, in addition to being the intersection of the main streets. Around the Forum the main streets of the town met, and we find the town's most important buildings.

The Arch of Nero.

The forum runs north-south for 142 metres and is 38 metres wide. As it had always been the seat of political and religious power, its buildings were frequently modified to reflect new construction techniques or fashions, cultural and political influences and also changes in cult worship.

The architecture in the Forum was characterised by a colonnade on three sides while the fourth side provided an uninterrupted view of the Temple of Jupiter. It was paved with travertine stone slabs, only a few traces of which now remain. Originally the colonnade consisted of a double order of Nuceria tuff-stone columns with Doric columns in the lower order and Ionic columns in the upper one. A few remains of these can be seen in the southern part of the Forum, while the western part preserves traces of the stairs leading up to the open gallery. The travertine stone colonnade was started in the Julio-Claudian age but was never completed. The bases of numerous statues are visible in the Forum. On these stood equestrian statues of emperors and influential citizens of the town and include the Suggestum, which was used for speaking to the townspeople. However, not a single statue was ever found. After the earthquake of 62 A.D. the Forum became a huge building site to repair the damage it had suffered and all the statues were transferred elsewhere. Moreover, it is thought that the Forum, like other parts of the town, was stripped of its marble and even its floor immediately after the eruption of 79 A.D. On either side of the Temple of Jupiter the Forum was closed by two arches topped with equestrian statues. The arch on the right-hand side is thought to be dedicated to Nero.

Aerial view of the Forum.

8 THE MUNICIPAL BUILDINGS

Three almost identical buildings situated on the southern side of the Forum were the seat of the town's municipal offices.
The most important of these were the Office of the *Duumviri*, the highest authority in the town, the Office of the *Aediles*, who were responsible for public works and maintenance of town buildings, the Council of *Decurions*, who acted as town councillors, and the municipal archives.
The first on the right, in the corner where the Basilica stands, was probably the Curia, seat of the *Ordo Decurionum* or town council.
The central building was probably the Office of the *Duumviri*. Finally, the third building has been attributed as the Office of the *Aediles*.

9 THE COMITIUM

In the corner where Via dell'Abbondanza enters the Forum we find a building that acted as a sort of polling station for municipal elections. The original building had no roof and could be reached via five entrances in the northern wall and five in the eastern one so that voters could enter from the Forum and go straight put into Via dell'Abbondanza. However, after the earthquake of 62 A.D. only three entrances were used: one in the north wall and two leading to the Forum. On the southern side of the building we find a podium where the magistrates sat when presiding over the electoral proceedings, while the other two walls contained niches housing honorary statues.

Comitium.

An "*honoured Pompeiian*"

In the later years which ended with the numbers "0" and "5" - every five years in effect, the *duoviri* elected took on the prestigious role of *quinquennalis,* having the powers which in Rome would have belonged only to the Censor *(taking the census of all citizens, updating electoral registers, deciding citizens' rights and naming new decurioni).*
Olconio Rufo was a real "*honoured Pompeiian",* so much so as to take on the role of *duumviro* five times, and that of *quinquennalis* twice.

View of the Municipal Buildings.

Town Administration

"PLEASE VOTE FOR HIM"

"O V F", (*oro vos faciatis* - "please vote for him") this was the customary abbreviation used at the end of a text of electoral propaganda painted on the walls. Hustings would be held in the town every March so that the electorate could decide which candidate to vote for in the April elections of the two *duumviri iure dicundo* and the two *aediles*, who would then take up office on the first of July. The *Duumviri* were the town's highest-ranking magistrates and were responsible for the political running of the town and the administration of justice. It was their job to ensure the implementation of the resolutions passed by what we can call the "town council" (*ordo decurionum*) which was made up of 100 members, elected every five years according to their status in terms of wealth and acknowledged honours. Less important tasks were carried out by the aediles who were responsible for the maintenance of public and religious buildings, the baths and the organisation of public games.

The **Comitium**, in the corner between the Forum and Via dell'Abbondanza, served as a polling station where the electorate (men only) would go during elections with their tesserula, a sort of polling card attesting to the voter's identity. Voters were required to write down the name of the chosen candidate on a waxed tablet which was then placed in the ballot box. The candidates that had attained the relative majority of votes in the most electoral constituencies would be elected. For instance, a candidate would not be elected if he got the maximum votes in just a few constituencies and no votes at all in the others. In the event of a tied vote, the winner would be chosen on the basis of whether he was married and how many children he had.

The whole town took a keen interest in the election campaign, as can be seen from the many inscriptions found on the walls. Every category of workers, traders and businessmen had a steadfast commitment to taking part as well as a strong sense of civic responsibility to ensure that the worthiest candidates were elected.

There must have been an almost full turn-out at every election, judging from the exhortations made on the electorate district by district, house by house and shop by shop. "Be careful, be ready and get others to vote" is the heartfelt appeal in one inscription; elsewhere, supporters of some candidate appeal to other voters and indicate the name of their candidate for whom they hope to gain support. Although women did not have the right to vote, they nevertheless played a crucial role given that they had a number of influential contacts through their work or social acquaintances.

Electoral slogans on the walls of Via dell'Abbondanza.

The electoral propaganda was written on the walls by the *"scriptores"* in response to a request not by the candidates themselves but by the people (ordinary citizens, corporations or local religious organisations) who intended to support the candidature of someone whom they considered worthy of holding public office.

10 THE BUILDING OF EUMACHIA

Continuing along the eastern side of the Forum, just after the junction with Via dell'Abbondanza, we find a majestic and elegant building with a marble friezc above the portal.

Two inscriptions - one on the marble colonnade in the Forum and another by the rear entrance in Via dell'Abbondanza - attribute this building to Eumachia, a priestess of Venus and owner of a flourishing business operating in the wool industry, which she had inherited from her husband.

Indeed, this is thought to be the seat of the Corporation of wool and cloth manufacturers.

The building itself dates from the Tiberian age and looks onto the Forum from a facade with two apses and four rectangular niches which, according to the fragments of inscriptions found here, housed the statues of the imperial family's ancestors: Aeneas, Romulus, Julius Caesar, the Emperor Augustus, as in the Augustan Forum in Rome.

Just inside the entrance, on the right we find a small room that was used as a urinal. Its location at the very centre of the Forum can be explained by the need to procure urine, which was used to bleach material in the manufacturing process.

A large courtyard inside the building was surroun-

The wool-makers dedicated a statue to the priestess, whose family manufactured tiles and amphorae and also made wine. The statue is on display at the National Archaeological Museum in Naples.

Detail of the sculpted marble portal.

The Building of Eumachia. The entrance from the Forum.

ded by a two-storey colonnade with an apse that housed a statue of the Concordia Augusta on a podium. On the other side of the colonnade wall with its large windows stood the three-sided cryptoporticus. Here, behind the apse the statue of Eumachia was found in a niche adjacent to a small corridor leading to Via dell'Abbondanza, right in front of the fountain that gives its name to the street (the Street of Plenty).

Damaged during the earthquake of 62 A.D. the building had been only partially restored by the time of the eruption.

The Building of Eumachia.
The room used for collecting urine.

The Building of Eumachia is thought to have been the seat of the Corporation of wool and cloth manufacturers. In the shelter provided by the colonnade, the products of Pompeii's businesses were traded while the materials were stored in the cryptoporticus behind.

11 THE TEMPLE OF VESPASIAN

Temple of Vespasian.

This temple was built after the earthquake of 62 A.D. as a place of worship for the cult of the emperor and has a facade projecting slightly further out than the building of Eumachia. A central door leads into a space in front of the inner sanctuary which is bounded on the front side by four columns. Inside these, a staircase on either side led up to a podium on which stood the cella containing the cult statue. Behind the sacellum were three rooms used for the officiators both of this temple and of the adjacent Temple of the Lares which could be reached via a communicating doorway. A marble altar with bas-relief sculptures can be seen in the centre of the sanctuary.

Temple of Vespasian. Imaginary reconstruction.

Altar of the Temple of Vespasian. The decoration on the front depicts a sacrificial scene with a bull being led towards the high-priest, portrayed with a veil on his head and pouring out libations on a tripod, set against a temple in the background.

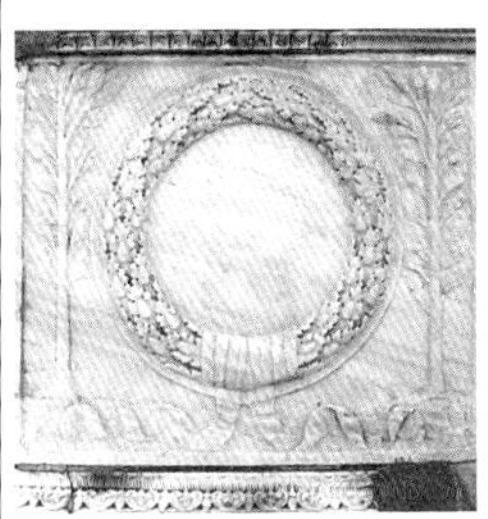

The side of the altar facing the cella portrays a crown of oak leaves and two bay trees.

The other two sides portray the sacred instruments used in the sacrificial rites.

12 THE TEMPLE OF THE PUBLIC LARES

This temple was built after the earthquake of 62 A.D. and was dedicated to Pompeii's tutelary gods as an act of expiation for the calamity the town had suffered. Although it had not been completed at the moment of the eruption, what remains suggests that its architecture was quite unusual. It was completely open on the side looking onto the Forum and could be reached through a portico adjoining the colonnade on the Forum, the bases of which are still visible.

13 MACELLUM

In the north-eastern corner of the Forum stood the covered market where the townspeople could buy the food they needed. Built during the Augustan age, its main entrances in the Forum and Via degli Augustali were lined with shops. It originally had a secondary entrance on Vico del Balcone Pensile which was later closed off when the Temple of the Public Lares was built.
The entrance under the colonnade in the Forum was divided into two gateways by a votive aedicula and led into the open space which was originally surrounded by a portico. A number of shops opened out onto the right-hand side of the Macellum.

The Forum colonnade, behind which stood the shops looking onto the Macellum.

The Macellum. In the centre we can see twelve bases which were used to support a wooden roof under which a fountain was provided for cleaning the fish sold in the market.

14 TEMPLE OF JUPITER

The name of the temple derives from its original function in the Samnite period.

Following the town's colonisation, the temple became a *Capitolium*, a temple dedicated to the capitoline triad of Jupiter, Juno and Minerva, in accordance with the religious tradition of Rome which required the centre of every town to have a temple dedicated to the most important gods on Mount Olympus. With its dominant position in the Forum and lofty Mount Vesuvius looming ominously behind it, the Temple of Jupiter is an emblematic image of the destruction of Pompeii.

A bas relief portraying the temple during the earthquake was found in the lararium in the house of *Caecilius Jucundus* and gives us a glimpse of what the building was really like.

The colossal torso of the statue of Jupiter.

The majestic architecture of the Temple of Jupiter which stands out against the impressive outline of Mount Vesuvius.

Civic Forum. Imaginary reconstruction of the Arch of Nero.

15 Public Toilets

Just beyond an area in which archaeological material is stored, we can see a room that led into the public toilets, an indispensable facility in a particularly busy town square. Built in the town's final years, the lavatory is provided with a drain running around three of the walls above which wooden or stone seats were fitted. As was customary for the time, the toilets were set one next to another, not in individual cubicles.

16 Grain Stores

This building is currently closed by a gate and is used for storing archaeological findings. Originally, it was a market where Pompeiians could buy cereals, herbs and dried pulses. It opened out onto the Forum and had evidently not been completed at the time of the eruption as the walls show no sign of having ever been plastered.

Mensa ponderaria. The stone block with cavities dug out of the counter corresponding to different weights.

17 Mensa Ponderaria

Nine round holes in a limestone block situated in a niche on the outer wall of the Temple of Apollo were used as standard measures. Here, under the supervision of the town magistrates, produce was weighed by placing it in the round cavities and then removed via the holes made below the counter. This public service had already been introduced in the Samnite period, but after 20 B.C. the measures - including three additional ones on a new counter - were adapted to the new parameters of the Roman system of weights and measures, as is explained on an inscription that the Duumviri had engraved on the stone block.

The Forum grain stores. Plaster cast.

18 Temple of Fortuna Augusta

Leaving the Forum now and heading along Via del Foro to the corner of Via della Fortuna, we find the Temple of Fortuna Augusta built at the expense of Marcus Tullius, a relative of the famous orator Cicero. This benefactor, an eminent citizen of Pompeii and twice Duumvir in the Augustan age, even went so far as to create the position of ministers of the cult. The temple thus acquired a political connotation, which was spread through the diffusion of the imperial cult. Hence whenever a new emperor succeeded to the throne, the ministers immediately had a statue built and placed in the temple along with a stone slab to commemorate the event.

The "sponsor" of the temple

Marcus Tullius is closely connected to the Temple of Fortuna Augusta, as can clearly be seen from the inscription: *Marcus Tullius, son of Marcus, Duumvir with jurisdictional power, thrice elected Augur and Military Tribune for five years in the name of the people, (erected) the Temple of Fortuna Augusta on his own soil and at his own expense.* In those times, this would have been seen as an operation with precise political ends. The Tullius family probably arrived in Pompeii during the time of Silla and reached the climax of their importance during the Augustan period. Records of this family have been found in various parts of central Italy, including Arpino, hometown of Cicero.

This fairly small building, which was destroyed during the earthquake of 62 A.D. and was never fully rebuilt, had the same architectural layout as the Temple of Jupiter.

Reconstruction.

THE THERMAL BATHS
A HEALTY REST

Stabian Baths.

The baths were generally subdivided into two sections: one for men and one for women, with separate entrances.
Usually, all the rooms in the baths were rigidly divided, starting from the changing rooms (*apodyterium*), in which clothes were left in wooden cupboards. Then the bathers passed into the *frigidarium*, for cold baths. This was followed by the *tepidarium*, heated up to a lukewarm temperature by braziers which were then used to prepare the hot baths. Finally, the bathers went into the *calidarium* with the pool for the hot bath in which there was a *labrum*, a small pool with cold water to refresh oneself.
Observation of the way the Roman baths worked has enabled us to find out many interesting things about their use of hydraulics and about construction techniques. The baths were heated using hot air which was circulated through a space in the walls made by a particular arrangement of the roof tiles (*tegulae mammatae*) and under the floor, raised up on small terracotta pillars (*suspensurae*). In some particularly well-equipped baths nearby, ovens were used to provide the necessary hot air and water.
Massages were also popular amongst bath-users, including the use of oils which were rubbed into the skin to protect it from the changes in temperature before and after going into the calidarium.
Before going into the thermal baths, gymnastics and swimming (in the places where a swimming pool was available, such as the Stabian baths) were usually practiced. Games were also popular, amongst which was a type of bowls. Visiting the baths had a real social function, seeing as they were an important meeting place.
They also show the amount of attention and care that the people of Pompeii dedicated to their own bodies.

Forum Baths. The men's Calidarium.

19 Forum Baths

These baths were situated in Via delle Terme in the building opposite the Temple of Fortuna Augusta. They were built in the first year of the founding of the colony with public funds and were always assiduously frequented by the town authorities. The damage suffered during the earthquake in 62 A.D. was immediately repaired, and they were in fact the only baths in use at the moment of the eruption in 79 A.D.

Although by no means a large establishment, the Forum baths were nevertheless equipped with all the bathing facilities that Roman citizens could desire.

A narrow corridor opening onto Via delle Terme led straight into the changing room and the entrances on Via del Foro and Vicolo delle Terme passed through a porticoed courtyard before reaching the changing room. The changing room had a barrel vault roof with a skylight in one of the lunettes, and both the walls and the vaults were embellished with stucco decorations on a yellow background, of which only a few traces now remain. The first chamber was the *frigidarium* a square shaped room lit by an opening in the vault, with apsidal niches in the corners and a round bath with steps in the centre of the room. The bathing chamber had a barrel vault ceiling while its walls were elegantly embellished with stucco work placed on either side of giants holding up a shelf. Lastly came the *calidarium* and, on the far wall, a marble *labrum*. The women's baths were laid out in a similar way on the other side of the boiler room, which was used by both sections, and could be reached from the entrance on Via delle Terme.

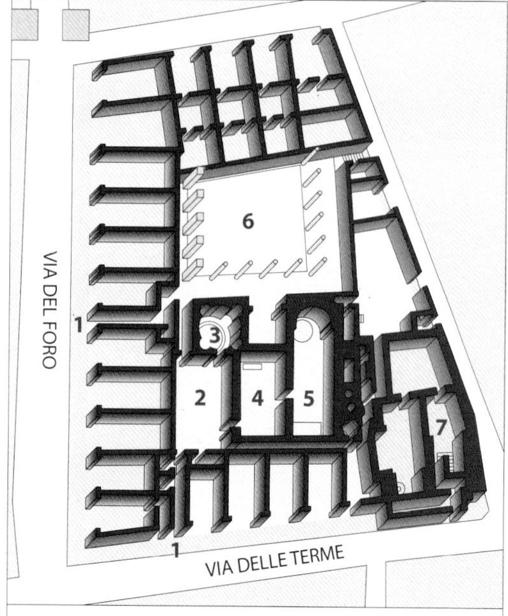

LAYOUT OF THE FORUM BATHS

1 - Entrances
2 - Apodyterium
3 - Frigidarium
4 - Tepidarium
5 - Calidarium
6 - Gymnasium
7 - Women's section

Tepidarium. The doorway through to the calidarium with niches on either side where customers could leave their clothes.

Seneca's description of the public baths

To get an idea of the public baths as they were around the middle of the 1st century B.C., we can do no better than to refer to an authoritative eye-witness who lived at that time: Seneca. In a letter he dictated the rules that had to be followed if a thermal complex was to satisfy the "ritual" content of a visit to the baths, and explained that bathers would only enjoy the experience "*if large circular mirrors were placed all round the walls; if Alexandrine marble was embellished with Numidian marble ornamentations; if artistic mosaics in various designs were provided in addition to those marble decorations; if the ceiling was made of glass; if marble from Thasos, which once could only be admired in temples, was used to encircle the tubs in which the bathers used to recover from the extenuating sweating process; and if the water flowed from silver taps*".

Frigidarium of the male section of the baths.

20 THE HOUSE OF THE TRAGIC POET

A mosaic depicting a growling dog and the well-known words of warning cave canem (beware of the dog) is the decoration found near the entrance of this medium-sized, imperial style house opposite the Forum baths. The house has a *Tuscan atrium* and a *peristyle* with a *lararium* situated on the rear wall. The *atrium* leads into the *cubicula* (bedrooms) and the *tablinum*. The house derives its name from a fine mosaic with a theatrical scene which was found in this *tablinum* along with paintings representing episodes from the Iliad. These finds are now exhibited at the National Archaeological Museum in Naples. To the right of the *peristyle* we find the *triclinium* whose frescoes and figured panels are still intact. The panel on the rear wall depicts Ariadne abandoned by Theseus while the panel on the left-hand wall portrays a nest full of cupids.

The House of the Tragic Poet. Reconstruction.

21 THE HOUSE OF THE LARGE FOUNTAIN

The garden of this house is embellished with a large fountain decorated with coloured mosaics and compositions made of glass paste tiles. Rows of shells running all round the nymphaeum form a highly original decoration which is completed by two large theatrical masks embedded in the bases of two columns. The water for the fountain flowed through a hole in the middle of the apse and fell over a flight of marble steps, creating an impressive effect, before being collected in a small pool decorated with a bronze statue of a cupid carrying a dolphin on his back. The statue on display here is a copy.

22 THE HOUSE OF THE SMALL FOUNTAIN

The garden of the adjoining house, called the House of the Small Fountain, has large landscape paintings and a smaller fountain with decorations very similar to the ones in the previous house. Here the water flows out from a marble mask of Silenus.

The House of the Large Fountain. The ornate fountain.

A panel with dice players. This painting was found in one of the rooms of the inn (according to some a gambling den) just opposite the fountain of Mercury.

The House of the Small Fountain.

23 THE TOWER OF MERCURY

From the top of this tower we can see the ruins of Pompeii from their highest point. This is one of the towers that were built into the town walls after the 3rd century as a vantage point from which to observe the whole town. In addition to the ground floor, it has two upper floors and a large embattled terrace from which patrols would set out for their rounds along the walls. The imprints left by the round stones hurled at the town by the catapults of Silla's army (90 B.C.) are still visible on the wall between the Porta Ercolano and the Porta Vesuvio gates. Two additional towers were later added to this section of the town walls.

A view of Via di Mercurio with the Tower in the background.

24 House of Apollo

This was the house of a rich Pompeiian merchant and takes its name from some pictures and a bronze statuette of Apollo. In the garden there is a fountain in the form of a pyramid. The house is laid out according to a symmetrical architectonic plan and - as much as can be seen from what is left must have been beautifully decorated.

25 House of Meleagrus

The name of this house derives from a picture - now hardly visible - showing Meleagrus and his bride Atalanta.
There is an interesting and unusual marble table with its legs in the form of winged gryphons and branches.

26 House of the Labyrinth

This is a large house with a double atrium and a private baker's (equipped with three millstones and an oven) annexed to it.

The house takes its name from a depiction of Theseus killing the Minotaur.
The Corinthian-style columned saloon with ten columns built into the walls is worth seeing.

Peristyle of the House of Meleagrus.

THE GARDENS OF POMPEII

The internal areas designated as gardens occupied a prime place in the Pompeiian house, and developed continuously during all periods of the city's evolution. In the older dwellings, built in the third and fourth centuries B.C., the open space was reserved for growing fruit and vegetables, necessary produce for day-to-day life. In the centuries that followed, it was transformed into the *viridarium* (garden), with an essentially ornamental character, which eventually became the focal point of the house with the creation of the columned portico (*peristilium* or *peristyle*).

Where there was not sufficient space for a complete *peristilium*, the private side of the portico had walls decorated with pictures of natural scenes, often framed by false colonnades to give the illusion of enlarging the actual dimensions of the green space. Hunting scenes, fights between wild animals and exotic landscapes also appeared, expanding the limited domestic dimension into an apparently unconfined natural space.

The architectonic design of the garden was completed by the widespread use of sculptures, decorative masks, *oscillae* (large hanging discs which "oscillated" in the wind), ponds and fountains with water games. Pollens, seeds, roots and the remains of carbonised fruit help us to understand which kinds of plants were cultivated; those which filled the gardens were not only ornamental, such as oleanders, hedges and box-trees, but many were also used for cosmetic and medicinal purposes in everyday life. Pomegranates, figs, vines, cherries and a few rare limes often shadowed the triclinia during the hot summer days.

A short walk through the gardens of Pompeii, recently restored, can be made by visiting some of the houses in which there a good view of the *viridaria*.

The Garden of the House of the Faun.

A view of the atrium with its impluvium.

An imaginary reconstruction of the atrium.

27 THE HOUSE OF THE FAUN

Covering a total surface area of about three thousand square metres, this building occupies a whole *insula* (block) and is certainly one of the largest and most sumptuous houses in Pompeii. Its entrance lies in Via della Fortuna.

The residence is of Samnite origin and was built in the early 2nd century B.C. in place of an older construction. It derives its name from the small bronze statue of a dancing faun (a copy of which is exhibited here) which decorates the *impluvium* of the *Tuscan atrium*. Nothing is known about its owners.

From an architectural viewpoint this house is unique not only for its remarkable size, but also because it has two *atria*, two *peristyles*, four *triclinia* and a small bathing complex. Each of the two distinct parts of the house was arranged around an *atrium* of its own.

The first part, which has a *Tuscan atrium*, is identified by the greeting "*Have*" which appears both in a mosaic on the pavement and on the 1st style decorations of the entrance hall. This was certainly the residential section of the house, while the other, laid out around a *tetrastyle atrium*, was where the servants lived and worked.

Opposite the entrance to the residential section is a *tablinum* whose floor is decorated with a cube design in perspective. The skeleton of a woman car-

The bronze statue of the dancing faun.

rying jewels and coins was found in this room and is assumed to have been the wealthy owner of the house. The house has two winter *triclinia*, one on either side of the *tablinum*, and a first *peristyle* with 28 stuccoed columns just behind the *tablinum* itself.

Two columns mark the entrance to the *exedra* in which the magnificent mosaic depicting a scene from the battle of Issus between Alexander the Great and King Darius of Persia was found.

A corridor from one of the two summer *triclinia* which extend all round the *exedra* leads to a larger *peristyle* with 48 Doric columns. This has a *lara-*

A detail from the famous mosaic of the battle of Issu between Alexander the Great and King Darius of Persia. I is probably the copy of a Hellenistic painting and is mad from over one and a half million tiles. It is now exhibited a the National Archaeological Museum in Naples.

Floor of the tablinium decorated with a pattern of cubes in opus sectile and, in the backgrou

rium on the left and the door to the gardener's lodgings on the right.
A secondary entrance to the house from Vicolo di Mercurio also leads into this *peristyle*.
In the servants' quarters, which can be reached through separate doors from two shops, we can see a number of *cubicula* where the staff slept.
The kitchen, the lavatory and the small private baths of the house opened onto a narrow passageway leading to the peristyle.
The baths are composed of a *tepidarium* and a *calidarium* which used the heat generated by the hearth in the adjoining kitchen and both had slightly raised floors.

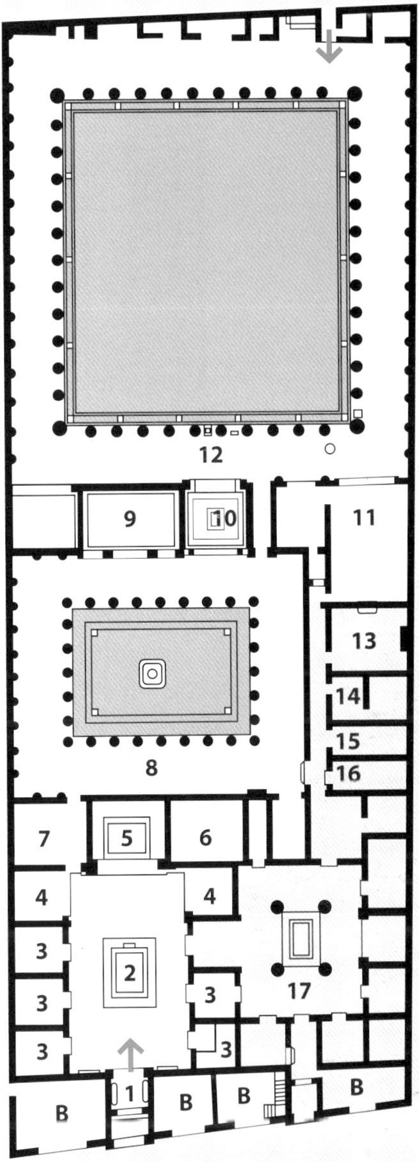

ntrance to the second peristyle.

Layout of the House of the Faun

1 Vestibulum	**11 Triclinium**
2 Atrium	**12 Peristyle**
3 Cubiculum	**13 Kitchen**
4 Alae	**14 Baths**
5 Tablinum	**15 Toilet**
6 Triclinium	**16 Stable**
7 Triclinium	**17 Atrium**
8 Peristyle	
9 Exedra	**B Shops**
10 Oecus	

Life in Pompeii

HOME SWEET HOME!

Generally speaking, the residential buildings in Pompeii are one-family houses with no upper floor and are completely sealed off from their surroundings. Their rooms are arranged in a hierarchical pattern round a central courtyard called the *atrium*. The house was lit through an opening in the roof of the *atrium* called the *compluvium*. The rainwater was collected in a pool called the *impluvium*, positioned right under the *compluvium*, and from there it was made to flow into an underlying cistern where it was stored. A narrow hallway called the *fauces* provided access to the house which was often flanked by *tabernae* (shops) opening directly onto the street.

The *atrium* is an inner courtyard open to the sky. When the surrounding roof has no supporting pillars, the *atrium* is said to be of the *Tuscan type*, if it has four supporting pillars it is called a *tetrastyle atrium*, and if there are more than four pillars it is said to be of the *Corinthian type*. A number of smaller rooms, usually *cubicula* (bedrooms) or store-rooms, were situated on either side of the *atrium*. The *tablinum* was usually positioned opposite the main door and was both the most important and the most "sacred" part of the house, being used both for reception purposes and as the hub of family life. The family's archives and the images of its forefathers were kept in the *alae* - two rooms positioned on either side of the *atrium*. The larger houses had a back garden which could be reached through a hallway from the *atrium* and was mainly used to grow vegetables to meet the needs of the family.

In the 2nd century B.C. the average size of the house increased as a result of the influence of Hellenistic construction techniques. In place of the vegetable garden the Romans began to build a *peristyle*, i.e. a colonnade, and would decorate the garden with sculptures and fountains and arrange the remaining living rooms all around it. Another type of Pompeiian building is the one used simultaneously for residential and commercial purposes. In this kind of house the ground-floor

usually comprised a shop looking onto the street and a back-room and was possibly completed by one or two upper floors.
In the 2nd century, when the more affluent families of the town felt the need for more luxurious dwellings, they began to build themselves villas outside the town. These were so large that they exceeded the limits of a single *insula* and were designed according to architectural principles intended to establish a close relationship between the building and its natural surroundings. They were usually divided into a residential section proper and a rural section which was used in the running of farming activities.

STAGES IN THE CONSTRUCTION OF THE TOWN

Pre-Samnite Age (tuff-stone and sandstone, opus quadratum), 7th - 6th centuries B.C.

First Samnite Age (sandstone and volcanic material: opus quadratum and opus incertum), 4th-3rd centuries B.C.

Second Samnite Age (tuff-stone buildings with Hellenistic influences), 200-80 B.C.

1st Period of the Roman Colony - Republican and Augustan Ages (opus saccarium, quasi-reticulatum and reticulatum) 80 B.C. - 14 A.D.

Second Period of the Roman Colony - Age of Claudius and first Age of Flavius (opus mixtum and bricks) A.D. 14-79.

28 THE HOUSE OF THE VETTII

This luxurious residence houses an impressive collection of fresco decorations typical of the wall paintings in the houses of rich Pompeiian traders. The excavation techniques used made it possible to preserve, in almost all the rooms in the complex, the fourth-style figure paintings completed after the earthquake of 62 A.D. The brothers Aulus Vettius Restitutus and Aulus Vettius Conviva commissioned their fresco decorations from one of the leading artists' workshops so that their home would be not only a comfortable residence but also a "status symbol".

The house is divided into two areas: firstly, the part in which the family lived, laid out around the main *atrium* and the *peristyle* with its beautiful garden (this house does not have the *tablinum* which was traditionally built between the two, opposite the main entrance); and secondly, the part where the servants lived and worked, on the right of the entrance hall and centred around a small *atrium* with a *lararium*.

The wall facing the entrance (1) is decorated with a fresco of Priapus weighing his phallus on a pair of scales and a sheep with the attributes of Mercury, the god of financial income, which here serve to protect the house from bad luck and as propitiatory symbols of wealth. The *atrium* (3) is decorated with scenes depicting sacrifices, hunts and cupids while two strong-boxes are anchored to stone blocks in the floor. The decision to site them here can probably be explained by the desire of the masters of the house to underline their wealth and importance.

The rooms laid out on the left of the entrance hall are decorated with mythological subjects, which are described below.

On the right-hand wall in the first room (4) we can see a fresco depicting the **myth of Leander** swimming towards his beloved Hero, while the opposite wall portrays **Ariadne abandoned by Theseus** on Naxos. The next room (5) is decorated with frescoes depicting **the struggle between Cupid and Pan**, **Cyparissus** who is transformed into a cypress tree after killing a sacred stag

The peristyle of the House of the Vettii; the garden was embellished with statuettes, columns and fountains. Today it has been partly reconstructed.

The fresco of Priapus weighing his enormous phallus at the entrance to the house.
This was considered to be a propitiatory symbol of wealth.

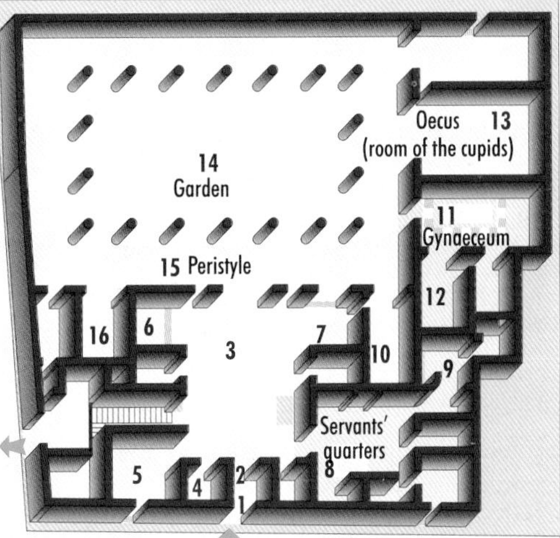

1	Vestibulum	10	Triclinium (room of Ixion)
2	Fauces	11	Gynaeceum
3	Atrium	12	Triclinium
4	Cubiculum	13	Oecus (room of the cupids)
5	Oecus	14	Garden
6-7	Alae	15	Peristyle
8	Servants' quarters	16	Oecus (room of Pentheus)
9	Kitchen		

Imaginary reconstruction of the peristyle and garden.

and, lastly, some images of Jupiter in the upper section of the wall. The two rooms (*alae*) (6-7) opening off the atrium just before it leads into the garden have frescoes painted on a yellow background; these depict a cock fight on the left, and two medallions portraying the heads of Medusa and Silenus on the right.
The *peristyle* (15) is decorated with black panelling with alternate still life and figure paintings. The garden (14) has been mostly rebuilt according to its original layout and was lavishly decorated with bronze and marble statuettes of cherubs and cupids, busts and heads on columns, tables, rectangular marble fountains along the four sides and round fountains in the four corners and in the centre.
Along the side of the *peristyle* facing the *atrium* we find two reception rooms that open onto the garden and are lavishly decorated with frescoes of mythological scenes set inside painted aediculae.
The living room on the left (16) just beyond the *atrium* has yellow painted walls with frescoes depicting: on the left, **Hercules strangling the serpents** sent by Juno; on the right **the punishment of Dirce** bound to the horns of a raging bull by Amphion and Zetus; while in the centre we see **the suffering of Pentheus** torn limb from limb by the Bacchanti.
The living room on the right (10) just beyond the *atrium* is decorated with a lower section of imitation coloured marble while, amidst an architectural flight of fancy, we can see: on the left, **Daedalus** presenting **Pasiphae** with the wooden cow in which she would hide as she was in love with a bull, and from whose union she

An erotic scene.

A room (7) with decorations on a yellow background.

Picture showing ricotta (soft cheese) and asparagus.

The lararium of the servants'quarters.

On the left: Hercules strangling the serpents and, on the right, the suffering of Pentheus.

was to give birth to the Minotaur; in the centre, the punishment inflicted on **Ixion** who is tied to a wheel built by Hephaestus and made to turn for all eternity as Hera sitting on the throne and Hermes look on; on the right, we can see **Bacchus watching Ariadne as she sleeps** on a tiger skin.
Leaving the living room and following the *peristyle* we find a few rooms set to one side and thought to have been reserved for women (*gynaeceum*) (11), where we can see a *triclinium* (12) and a *cubiculum* opposite a small garden.
Two frescoes in this area depict **Odysseus recognising Achilles**, and **Auge surprised by a drunken Hercules**.
The *triclinium* (13) runs in the same direction as the garden (which has been planted with the original aromatic herbs) and houses an extremely unusual miniaturised decoration above a lower panel.
This portrays **cupids** and their female equivalents (*psyches*) engaged in a number of different activities; from right to left these scenes depict: archery; arranging flowers and making floral crowns with roses carried by a billy goat; the manufacture and sale of perfumes; races with chariots drawn by antelopes; a

The room named after Ixion.

Detail from the paintings in the room of the cupids.

goldsmith's workshop; work in a dyer's shop.
On the rear wall we can see, again from right to left: bakers celebrating their tutelary god Vesta; wine-making; the triumphal procession of Bacchus lying on a cart pulled by billy-goats; the sale of wine.
The figure paintings which were here fastened to the wall by nails are now missing while the vermillion side panels depict well-known divine couples in flight. From the right, **Perseus and Andromeda**, **Dionysus and Ariadne**, **Apollo and Daphne**, **Neptune and Amymone** and, beside the entrance, **Silenus astonished by Hermaphroditos**.
Leaving the residential part of the house through a doorway beside the main entrance, we come into the area where the servants worked and lived. In the small *atrium* (8) we find the *lararium*, the altar to the domestic gods, on which we can see a scene depicting the Genius with two Lares dancing on either side above a serpent, the symbol of regenerative power. In the fireplace in the kitchen (9) we can see some tripods with 5 bronze pans and other containers, while in the adjoining room, which was reserved for the cook and was decorated with erotic paintings, we find a marble statue of Priapus that had originally been used as a fountain in the garden.

The room of the cupids is decorated with figures standing out against a red background.

The triclinium which runs in the same direction as the garden houses miniaturised decorations depicting cupids and their female equivalents (psyches) engaged in a number of different activities.

The styles of painting in Pompeii

Paintings to Inspire Dreams

The wall decorations in Roman houses have been subdivided into four styles.

The First Style, also called "encrustation style", was popular from 150 B.C. up to 80 B.C. and can be recognised by the shiny stucco decoration imitating the marble-lined walls.

1st style painting. The House of the Faun.

The Second Style, also referred to as the "architectural style", is characterised by the fact that for the first time the walls of the house are endowed with an illusion of being "open" to the outside world. This style was common between 80 B.C. and 14 A.D. and involved the depiction of architectures which extended the physical space of the house towards imaginary landscapes. The decoration does not merely attempt to imitate marble patterns but makes good use of perspective to create two or more levels of depth. These composition included columns in the foreground and colonnades in perspective disappearing into the distance with figure subjects or large paintings depicting a mythological, heroic or religious theme, in addition to small panels with doors set between the architectural features. This highly scenographic decoration seems to have been inspired by a growing theatrical taste. **The Third Style**, up to the year 62 A.D., abandons the use of space and architectural features as the subject matter of the composition with the result that the overall decoration loses depth. The columns, balustrades, architraves and shelves are flattened against the wall to conserve a purely ornamental function.

Columns are often used in an elongated form to frame large figure paintings inserted in large areas of plain-coloured wall. Landscapes are reduced to miniatures inserted into a single colour background, now painted in new shades of sea-green and golden yellow. The Third Style is also referred to as "pseudo-Egyptian" because of the presence of typically Egyptian elements: lotus flowers, small stars, rosettes, coloured fillets and a band running above the skirting with details of still life scenes, gardens with bullrushes and elegant birds in a variety of poses. This period is also responsible for the wall decorations depicting large-scale subjects inspired by gardens with trees, fountains, pools,

2nd style painting. The Villa of Mysteries.

3rd style painting. The House of Marcus Lucretius Fronto.

small columns and birds in flight. From the earthquake of 62 A.D. up to the town's destruction in 79 A.D., the houses in Pompeii were decorated with **Fourth Style** paintings. These were also said to be in the "ornamental style" because the whole wall is treated simply as a free ornamental composition. The architectural features no longer have any reference to reality and are reduced to unreal designs, a mere flight of fancy in which ornamentation is often excessive. There is also frequent use of bas-relief stucco work, as in the Second Style. Figure paintings become smaller or disappear altogether. Formal subjects are chosen, often inspired by philosophical or exotic themes, although we still find paintings that draw on the everyday life or news reports of important events, such as the brawl that took place in the Amphitheatre, the painting of which is now displayed at the National Archaeological Museum in Naples. The Fourth Style was a sign of wealth that typified the houses of the rich merchants of Pompeii before the catastrophe. This tendency drew inspiration from the models adopted in the Domus Aurea, the imperial palace in Rome, built after Nero had set fire to the capital in 64 A.D. destroying many buildings.

4th style painting. The House of Fabius Rufus.

29 THE HOUSE OF ARA MASSIMA

This house occupies a confined space in the inner part of an *insula*, or block. Its architectural structure and decorations serve to try and increase, or otherwise cover up, the space in which the house finds itself. This effect can be noted in the striking decorations on the wall at thc bottom of the atrium. The paintings which decorate the *tablinium* and the open-air *triclinium* are in the elegant fourth Pompeian style, and allusions to Dionisiac rites can be seen, the theatrical masks and cups with covered phalluses, for example.

The House of Ara Massima. Mars and Venus.

30 THE NECROPOLIS AT THE PORTA VESUVIO GATE

Several tombs have been excavated in a necropolis just outside the Porta Vesuvio gate. One worth special mention is the tomb of **Caius Vestorius Priscus**, one of the town's aediles who died at the age of 22. An inscription indicates that the tomb was built on ground donated by the decurions, who had contributed the sum of two thousand sesterces to cover the costs of his funeral.

View of the archaeological site from the Porta Vesuvio gate. On the right there is the tomb of Vestorius Priscus.

The tomb of Caius Vestorius Priscus.
This tomb is surrounded by a high wall with a central altar standing on a base containing the burial chamber. It is entirely decorated with frescoes depicting scenes of hunts and gladiatorial combat and also contains some examples of silverware. On the south side of the altar base there is a portrait of the deceased in his civic role as an administrator of justice.

31 Castellum Aquae

Near this important gateway to the villas and farms in the countryside to the north of Pompeii we find an example of hydraulic engineering work which was an important part of the town's water supply system.
This is the so-called *Castellum Aquae*, which channelled water from a branch of the Augustan aqueduct from Serino into three pipes to supply the different parts of the town.
This feat of engineering was extremely useful and marked a change in the people's habits as, prior to this, they had had to draw water from wells or use rainwater that had been channelled from the house's *impluvium* into specially built tanks.
In the town a dense network of small tanks was constructed, the so-called *castella acquaria*, usually brick-built and resting on high pillars, which also had the purpose of raising the pressure of the water which ran through lead tubes.
Up to today, 22 wells have been found, some of which were for public use. To reach the underground reservoirs it was necessary for the wells to reach a depth of some 30 metres.
The terrible earthquake of 62 A.D. also caused serious damage to the Castellum Acquae, as can be seen from the famous lararium in the house of Cecilius Jocondus, and at the moment of the eruption further outlets of the great cistern were being rebuilt. At other points however, temporary pipes have been found.

The city was connected to the Roman acqueduct by means of a diversion which entered Pompei at the highest point of the plane, where the Castellum Acquae had been purpose-built. The function of this cistern was to gather the large amounts of water coming from the acqueduct and direct them into the urban water system, controlling the flow through a system of movable doors.

A castellum aquaria just behind a public fountain.

32 House of the Gilded Cupids

The garden was lavishly decorated with statuettes, busts, animal sculptures and theatrical masks which were fitted into the walls and hung between the columns, in addition to medallions against the evil eye.

Opposite the house of the Vettii, in the triangular-shaped insula on Via Vesuvio, stands the house belonging to the wealthy *gens Poppaea* - possibly the family of Nero's second wife. The house obtained its name from the original decoration used for the *cubiculum* near the shrine of the tutelary gods, where, set into the plaster, there were several glass discs whose gold leaf back bore the engraving of the cupids.
The layout of the house is quite unusual as it has an *atrium* and *tablinum* but no *cubicula* (bed chambers) on either side, and all of this is off-set compared to the rest of the house, which elegantly extends out towards the *peristyle* and garden.
The colonnade - along which we find the *lararium* and, tucked away in one corner, the *sacellum* dedicated to the Egyptian triad of Harpocrates, Isis and Serapis - follows the slope of the ground so that the west-facing side is higher than the rest. Here we find the *triclinium* with its stone beds and two lavishly decorated rooms: the one on the left, with a vegetable garden to the rear, shows a depiction of the seasons against a white background, while the other (which backs onto the kitchen) is decorated with love-related themes, such as Leda and the swan, Venus fishing, and Actaeon spying on Diana while she bathes. Both rooms have particularly striking coffered ceilings.

The original decoration in the cubiculum where the gilded cupids were found.

33 House of the Silver Wedding

This house was named in honour of the Italian royal couple, Umberto and Margherita of Savoy, on the occasion of their silver wedding anniversary in 1893, the same year in which the house was discovered.
It is located in the last side street off Via Vesuvio, next to an area which has yet to be excavated.
It was built in the 2nd century B.C. and is distinguished by its high atrium with four large Corinthian columns which support the roof, and its bedroom where the sunlight was filtered by means of veils. There are two gardens. The first is in line with the *atrium* and has its own private bath-house and open-air swimming pool, a large kitchen and garden and an elegant living room. The latter was decorated with a mosaic floor and second style paintings and has four octagonal imitation porphyry columns supporting a barrel-vaulted ceiling.

Cubiculum decorated in the second style.

The impressive tetrastyle atrium of the Home.

The room with octagonal imitation porphyry columns.

34 THE HOUSE OF CAECILIUS JUCUNDUS

This house on Via Vesuvio, with its classical layout around an *atrium* and a *peristyle*, belonged to the banker of Pompeii, and his entire archives consisting of 154 waxed writing tablets dating between 53 and 62 A.D. were found intact. These consisted of sale contracts for land, animals or slaves and receipts for the payment of colonial ta-xes, as Lucius Caecilius Jucundus was also the official tax collector. The bronze portrait - commissioned from the freedman Felix - found in the *tablinum* of the house gives us a clear image of what his father looked like. In this house, researchers found two marbles bas-reliefs (both subsequently stolen). One of them depicts the temple of Jupiter wich was damaged during he earthquake of 62 A.D., and the relevant expiatory sacrifice.

35 TABERNA LUSORIA

In the façade of this house, also known as the *"Bisca Lusoria"*, or Gaming House of the Luxuries, there is a tufo bas-relief showing two coupled phalluses with a cup used for playing dice between them.
The building was damaged by bombing in 1943.

Detail from the paintings which decorated the tablinium of the house.

Bronze portrait of the father of Caecilius Jucundus.

36 CENTRAL BATHS

The degree of importance of thermal bathing houses in Pompei can be understood from looking at the construction of the Central Baths. After the 62 A.D. earthquake an entire *insula* (or block) at the crossroads between the via di Nola and the via di Stabia was used as the site upon which to build the new thermal complex. The construction of the baths was never finished due to the additional devastating effect of the eruption of Vesuvius in 79 A.D..

Bas-relief sign from the Lusoria Tavern.

THE STREETS

The streets of Pompeii vary in width from 2.5 to 4.5 metres and are made from large slabs of Vesuvian lava, while the pavements, which are usually around 30 centimetres high, were surfaced with a mixture of broken terracotta and fat lime cement, most of which has been worn away by the millions of visitors. One interesting feature is the so-called "pedestrian crossings", made from stone slabs of equal height to the pavement, placed across the street. These allowed pedestrians to cross the road without getting their feet wet or dirty as the streets were often filthy due to the lack of a proper sewer network. However, the slabs were placed in such a way that carts could still pass, as can be seen by the ruts left in the road by the cartwheels.

In keeping with the definitions given to the street layout of Greek cities the term "*decumanus*" is also used in Pompeii to describe the main streets running from west to east, and "*cardo*" for the streets generally running from north to south to connect up the various *decumani*.

The original names of the streets were in the Oscan language, such as **via Sarina**, from Forum to **veru Sarinu** (Port of Salt) - the original name for what is now known as "Porta Ercolano" - in a reference to the *Salinae Herculae* salt works on the coast towards Oplontis. The streets **via Iùviia**, **via Pùmpaiiana**, and **via Dekkurium** or **Decuviare** were built around the middle of the 2nd century B.C. by the *aediles*, all belonging to the Samnite aristocracy, and whose names come from the street signs that have been discovered.

37 House of the Centenary

This large house, built in the 2nd century B.C. and restructured during the Imperial age, opens onto Via di Nola and was given this name as it was discovered in 1879, the year of the eighteenth centenary of the eruption which completely buried Pompeii. It is divided into two sections: the main house, for the master's family, and the servants' quarters, with a separate entrance from a side street. In line with tradition it has a private bath-house and swimming pool.
There is also a particularly beautiful *nymphaeum* with a fountain situated at the rear of the *peristyle*, and a bed chamber in the eastern section of the house which is decorated with two highly detailed erotic frescoes.

Painting from the lararium showing Bacchus and Mount Vesuvius resplendent with vineyards.
Below: one of the two erotic paintings which decorated a private bed chamber.

38 House of Marcus Lucretius Fronto

The house itself is well known for its refined third style decorations, which are considered to be superior to those found in Rome. The juxtaposition of shiny black walls with interposed yellow bands depicting arabesques and hunting scenes, and the black floor with inlaid pieces of marble is particularly unusual. The decorations in the *tablinum* are worth close examination and depict landscapes with villas and gardens as well as two mythological paintings. The wall to the left illustrates the marriage of Venus and Mars while to the right we can see the Triumph of Bacchus accompanied by Ariadne on a carriage drawn by oxen. In the yellow room to the right of the *tablinum*, there is a painting on the left between a group of cupids which depicts Narcissus looking at his reflection in the water and, on the

Tuscan atrium decorated with 3rd style paintings and the tablinum in the background.

Landscape with sea-side villas.

right, Perona breastfeeding her old father, Myconis. In the centre of the left wall in the winter *triclinium* (immediately after the v*estibulum*) there is an illustration of a scene taken from Euripides' tragedy Andromache, in which Neottoleus is killed by the sword of Orestes on the altar of Apollo. In the next *cubiculum* there is a 'triumph' of extremely small and intricate details set against a black background, while on the right wall there is a painting of Ariadne bringing Theseus the thread so that he can find his way through the labyrinth. The house extends out towards the back garden, whose walls used to be covered in frescoes depicting hunts for wild beasts and other animals.

The marriage of Mars and Venus.

39 House of M. Obellius Firmus

This house dates back to the Samnite period and was being restored when the volcano erupted. It is built around two *atriums* and a section of *peristyle* with a garden. The main *atrium* is tetrastyle. There is a table on a pedestal (*cartibulum*) in front of the entrance, between the *impluvium* and the large *tablinum*, whereas the *lararium* is situated in the first right-hand corner. A bronze safe - a clear sign of the family's wealth - is solidly anchored to the ground near the living room (*alae*) on the right-hand side of the house. In addition to the fact that it has a *tablinum*, the importance of the house is also expressed by the size of the reception hall alongside it, opening out onto the peristyle through a wide doorway. A plaster cast of the door is on display. The secondary *atrium*, which is Tuscan and has no columns, is linked to both the first atrium and the *peristyle*. The *tablinum* is situated in this part of the house and is decorated with second style paintings, while the kitchen, which is hidden behind the corridor leading to the *peristyle*, is annexed to the bath-house which was heated by the kitchen oven. The house extends towards the garden and the peristyle with its three-sided colonnade, where the reception rooms and sleeping areas are much smaller and still bear some traces of the fine wall decorations.

Imaginary reconstruction of the atrium in the house.

This was the last house on Via di Nola to be entirely unearthed.

40 THE PORTA DI NOLA GATE AND THE NECROPOLIS

The Porta di Nola gate, built at the end of one of the main town roads, is situated on the edge of the hill of Pompeii. It is a square-shaped gate with two projecting structures, a barrel vault, and an effigy of Minerva on the inside. A necropolis was found at the foot of the town walls outside the gatc where excavation work has uncovered several particularly interesting burial monuments. There are three tombs, two of which are semicircular exedrae made of tuff stone with two paws of winged lions poised on the far ends. One tomb belonged to the wife of a *duumvir*, Aesquillia Polla, who died at the age of 22. In the other tomb, surrounded by a wall, was buried Marcus Obellius Firmus, who had been elected several times to the position of town administrator. In the same part of the town archaeologists found an area which presumably was where the deceased were cremated, in addition to four graves - identified by the funerary steles - of Pretorian soldiers stationed in Pompeii.

Marble tombstone of M. Obellius Firmus.

Semicircular exedra tomb.

Via di Nola and porta di Nola gate.

41 THE HOUSE OF THE ANCIENT HUNT

On Via della Fortuna, a short distance from the House of the Faun heading towards the Porta di Nola gate, we find a house named after the large and evocative fresco on the garden wall depicting a mountain landscape where an ancient hunt for wild beasts is in progress. It is a house of Samnite origin and contains some fine examples of fourth style decoration. Personifications of autumn and winter are depicted on the walls of the *atrium*, while the facing walls of the second *cubiculum* on the right portray mythological subjects.

On the left we can see Leda and the swan, portrayed amid medallions with the busts of Jupiter and Diana and, on the right, Venus fishing between Mercury and Apollo. In the *tablinum* we find Nile landscapes with Pygmies, cherubs hunting wild beasts and a highly effective depiction of carpets and pieces of cloth billowing in the wind. The *exedra* opposite the garden is embellished with fantastic architectures and lavish ornamental motifs in which we can see Diana bathing as Actaeon watches, and Apollo in the background with a shepherd.

The tablinum: small pictures portraying scenes of cupids hunting wild beasts.

Tablinum decorations.

42 THE BAKERY OF MODESTUS

The eighty-one round loaves found carbonised in this building, already divided into eight slices, were ready to be sold before they were buried. As well as the oven, a grain store and another store, on the left, for previously baked bread can be found here.

A charred loaf of bread.

A painting of a bakery.

Modestus' bakery was one of the thirty bakeries active in Pompeii.

43 THE LUPANAR (BROTHEL)

The Lupanar was the official brothel of Pompeii. As a trading town, it was visited every day by large numbers of people, especially traders from other towns. The brothel is situated at the intersection of two side roads on Via dell'Abbondanza near the town centre, not far from the Forum and the Stabian Baths (which had a rear entrance on the Vicolo del Lupanare).

Phalluses engraved on the basalt road surface or on stones set into the facades of houses gave visitors clear indications on how to reach the brothel.

We find explicit reference to the use to which this building was put, unlike many other brothels in the town (there were probably 25 in all) which were situated on the first floor above taverns and houses. The lupanar had ten stone beds with mattresses, each bed set in its own small room. Five of these were found on the ground floor, while the larger rooms were situated on the first floor which could be reached by an independent entrance and a wooden staircase.

To the right of the entrance on the ground floor, the wall has a painting of Priapus depicted with two phalluses, one in each hand, while on the doors to the rooms we find illustrated scenes of sexual acts advertising the "specialities" of the resident prostitutes.

The customers expressed their opinions of the brothel and the performance of the prostitutes by scratching them on the walls, as can be seen by the approximately 120 examples of explicit graffiti. The brothel was managed by a "*leno*" (an owner of prostitutes) who bought the girls as slaves, primarily in the East at an average price of 600 *sesterces*. The brothel's tariffs varied from 2 to 16 asses (1 as was equal to about half a sesterce).

Small room with brick-built bed.

Priapus with two phalluses holding his twin attributes in both hands.

Erotic scenes depicting the "specialities" of the resident prostitutes.

UNINHIBITED EROS

Love was a common topic of conversation in Pompeii. Feelings, passions, poetic love, sex, homosexuality, prostitution and so forth were all part of daily life and not a source of prejudice. The concept of "obscenity" seems to have been unknown.

Love and sex were considered earthly practices of a man's life that were encouraged by the benevolence of Venus.

Among the thousands of examples of graffiti found on the town's walls there are several colourful and somewhat explicit examples of what the people of Pompeii thought about love and sex.

Pompeii was thus held to be the town of Venus, the goddess of love and the regenerative force in nature to whom Silla dedicated the colony.

We therefore find several places of cult worship dedicated to the goddess, and she is also the subject of many paintings and poetic graffiti found scratched into the walls.

In the Basilica we find clear proof of this in an inscription: "*If you are looking for sweet embraces in this town, you will find that all the girls here are available*".

The town had numerous brothels, or "*lupanares*", with young women from every part of the empire, each one specialised in a particular sexual technique.

Rooms for sexual encounters were also to be found in many taverns, baths and even ordinary houses which sometimes had rooms decorated with erotic frescoes for the sexual entertainment of guests.
The use of phallic symbols in frescoes, sculptures, charms, lamps, and in many corners of the town's houses, on the facades of the buildings and at the entrance to shops was very common. Surprisingly, these actually referred to magical practices as the phallus was considered the primordial positive force in nature and, thus, the main and most effective amulet against the evil eye and a sure way of ensuring health and well-being.

44 THE STABIAN BATHS

The town's oldest baths complex opens onto Via dell'Abbondanza at the corner of Via Stabiana and probably dates from the 2nd century B.C..

The establishment covers a total surface area of over 3,500 square metres includes a courtyard which was used as a gymnasium. Three sides of the courtyard have colonnades (P) with stuccoed tuff-stone pillars, while the fourth side borders onto a large swimming-pool one and a half metres deep (3). Separated from the gymnasium by a low wall, the latter could be reached from two side-rooms (2-4) where the bathers would probably get changed for the bathing rite.

After the earthquake of 62 A.D. the swimming-pool area was embellished with elegant coloured stucco decorations which enclose a number of panels depicting mythological figures and athletes. Only a few bathing chambers were annexed to the gymnasium to the north. The other rooms were later turned into a large lavatory (6) situated at the rear of the apartment belonging to the manager of the baths.

The bathing establishment proper occupies the longer side of the peristyle. A door in the right-hand corner of the colonnade (7) leads to the men's section. The first room on the left is a chamber for cold baths (*frigidarium*) (10), which is round in shape with four corner niches and a pool in the centre. The water used to feed the pool flowed from another niche in the north-facing wall. The fact that this room came before the one where the bathers un-dressed may suggest that it was actually used as a *laconicum*, i.e. a steam room in which the air was heated by means of bron-ze bra-

The coloured stuccoes of the barrel vault in the entrance hall of the men's section.

The gymnasium colonnades. As the gymnasium is situated in the older core of the 4th century complex, it is generally assumed that the building was originally a palaestra and was changed into a thermal establishment only in the 2nd century. B.C.

The layout of the Stabian Baths

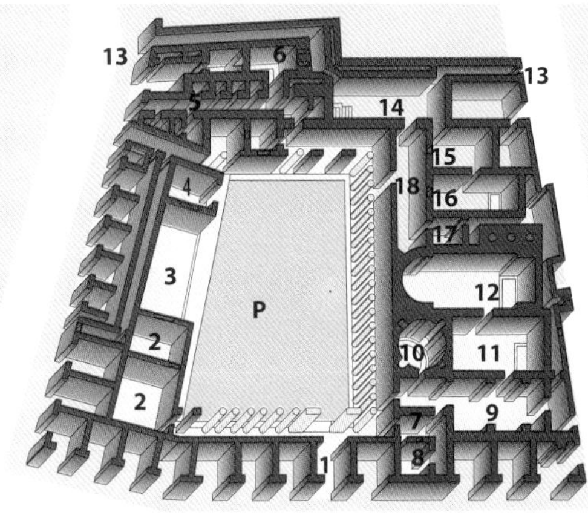

Via dell'Abbondanza

COLONNADED COURTYARD
P Gymnasium
1 Entrance
2 Swimming pool wash basins
3 Swimming pool
4 Swimming p. changing room
5 Individual bathing chambers
6 Toilets

MEN'S SECTION
7 Entrance
8 Waiting-room
9 Changing-room
10 Frigidarium
11 Tepidarium
12 Calidarium

WOMEN'S SECTION
13 Entrance
14 Changing-room
15 Tepidarium
16 Calidarium
17 Laconicum
18 Walking-area

ziers. From the entrance hall the bather entered the changing room (*apodyterium*) (9), which is plastered in white except for a red band running all round the lower half of the walls; the vault has stucco decorations in various colours. The next room is the *tepidarium* (11). The room that follows is the *calidarium* (12) where the tub on the right-hand side was used for hot baths. Abovc the bath we can see three niches which contained statues while the marble basin situated along the apsidal wall contained cold water which the bathers used to cool off while in that intensely heated room. Thc fircs for heating both the water and the air needed for the two sections of the bathing complex were situated behind the calidarium wall. Walking along the gymnasium colonnade, we reach the entrance door to the women's section (13).

Here the rooms follow one another in the same sequence as in the men's section, but as there is no *frigidarium*, the bathers would pass directly from the changing room (14) into the *tepidarium* (15) and from there to the *calidarium* (16).

The entrance to the Stabian baths.

45 TEMPLE OF ISIS

Just behind the Large Theatre we find the Temple of Isis with its entrance in the street of the same name (Via del Tempio di Iside). Originally dating from between the late 2nd and early 1st centuries B.C., it was totally rebuilt after the earthquake of 62 A.D. at the expense of an ex-slave (*libertus*) who had since made his fortune.

As he could not himself enter the Council of Decurions he had the work carried out in the name of his six-year-old son, as is explained in an inscription on the entrance to the temple: "*Numerius Popidius Cel-sinus, son of Numerius, at his own expense entirely rebuilt the Temple of Isis which had collapsed during the earthquake. In view of such generosity the decurions admitted him to their assembly free of charge, even though he was only six years old*".

The cult of Isis became fairly widespread during the Hellenistic era due to the religious links the Greeks had with Egypt and

Imaginary reconstruction of the Temple of Isis.

Statue of Isis.

View of the Temple of Isis.

the Orient, and it had a particularly large following in Pompeii.
The temple stands on a tall podium situated in the centre of a porticoed courtyard. Behind the temple there is a large meeting room which was probably used during preparations for the rites. Excavation work between the entrance columns unearthed a marble hand, a golden goblet, a statuette, two bronze candlesticks, and two human skulls, which were probably used in cult rituals. To the sides of the room there are two other rooms which were obviously connected with the cult as four wooden statues with marble heads, hands and feet were found in one of them. In front of the temple in the left-hand corner of the portico we find a room that was designated for purification ceremonies (*purgatorium*) where water from the river Nile was kept in containers in the basement underneath.

46 Samnite Gymnasium

Here it was discovered a statue of Doriphorus, the symbol of youth and strength and a Roman copy of the original by Polycletus. More than a *gymnasium* (palaestra) however, it was actually the headquarters of a military association of noble Pompeiian youths.
Opposite the entrance there are two pedestals, the largest of which most probably housed the statue of Doriphorus.

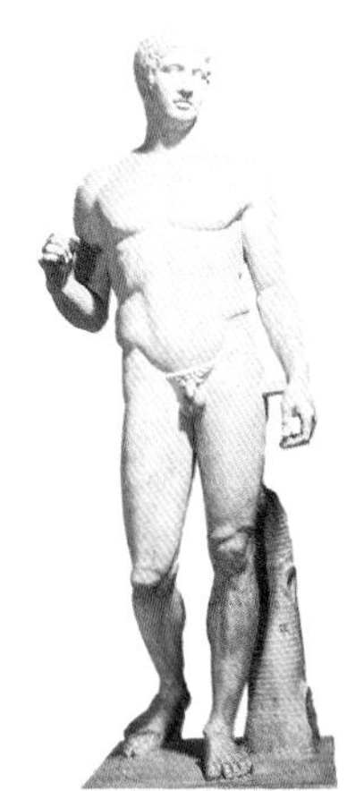

The marble statue of Doriphorus, currently in the N. Archaeological Museum in Naples.

The building dates back to the 2nd century B.C. and is enclosed by tuff-stone Doric columns on three sides only as, after the earthquake of 62 A.D., the nearby Temple of Isis was extended into the gymnasium area.

Religious Beliefs

FROM THE PHALLUS TO ISIS

In Pompeii, **Venus** was worshipped as the creator of the universe since it was she who meted out life and death; she was the "*Venus Pompeiana*" (Venus of Pompeii) and also mother nature (*Venus Physica*) and the goddess of fertility and abundance. Other popular cults included that of **Apollo** (the main god worshipped in Pompeii in the 6th century B.C.) and the cult of the Capitoline triad of **Jupiter, Juno** and **Minerva**, whose temple, or "*Capitolium*" stood to the north of the forum.

Bronze pendant with a large phallus 'used' as an amulet.

The Pompeiians also honoured the divinities who watched over the goods which were transported by sea and along the river Sarno. Outside Pompeii, near the town's river port, a sanctuary was erected to **Neptune** and a votive shrine was found there along with an inscription. Of course, the cult of the emperor was also widespread, and in particular his "Genius" and his "Fortune" were revered. The Temple of Fortuna Augusta was erected, while a temple was built and dedicated to the "**Genius of Vespasian**" in a small area of the Forum itself. Nearby, a **Temple to the Public Lares** was built, probably after the earthquake of 62 A.D.. It was dedicated to the protectors of the town in order to regain their goodwill and placate their anger as, according to popular belief, this had been responsible for the terrible calamity.

Frequent contact with the East led to the importation of rites involving orgies, which were dedicated in particular to **Isis**. A temple was erected to the Egyptian goddess in the theatre district and several houses in Pompeii bear witness to her cult. In the so-called "*House of Magical Rites*", dedicated to the god Sabatius, some inte-

Via dell'Abbondanza. The Venus of Pompeii amid flying cupids.

resting finds include two bronze "magic hands" and two sacrificial vases.
Lastly, evidence of the cult of the "*Magna Mater*", the great goddess **Cybele** or the "Great Mother of the Gods" who was associated with fertility and fecundity, can be seen in popular paintings such as those in a felt-makers' shop in Via dell'Abbondanza.
In any case the religious nature of the inhabitants of Pompeii was clearly visible in the cult of the **Lares**, to whom an altar was also dedicated.
The tutelary deities of the house were originally the spirits of the ancestors who in various paintings were often accompanied by the "**Geniuses**", the symbols of the procreating strength of the head of each family. The most popular simulacra of the town's divinities can be seen in some of the paintings discovered here, but they were more often represented in bronzes placed on altar shelves. Libations were frequently offered to them during meals in order to obtain their favour.
Practices against the evil eye and every kind of disease in favour of health, fertility and love were very common, as is indicated by thc various amulets discovered around the town.
The most popular amulet among the Pompeiians was the phallus. It was reproduced in every possible manner, from paintings and bas-reliefs to pendants, and could be found every-where: on the walls of houses, at the entrances to shops, on fountains and even inside houses.

Via dell'Abbondanza. Bas-relief depicting the phallus in a small temple.

Mercury in a small Etruscan-style temple.

The "magical hands" are represented in the act of blessing, with ring finger and little finger folded, and the god Sabatius appearing in the palm is surrounded by the symbols of various divinities: the pine-cone of Attis, the caduceus of Mercury and the cymbal and tympanum of Cybele.

The procession of Cybele and the god Dionysus in the niche.

47 THE TRIANGULAR FORUM

This building is clearly visible from the sea as it is situated on the promontory of the hill of Pompeii. Passing along Via dell'Abbondanza to the end of Via dei Teatri we find a portico with three Ionic columns and a semicolumn which form the entrance to the Triangular Forum. The Hellenistic style arrangement of the area, which has a colonnade with 95 columns, dates back to the 2nd century B.C.. The Doric Temple was built using limestone from the Sarno valley during the mid 6th century B.C. and was dedicated to Hercules, although it was later also adopted for the cult of Minerva. However, it was abandoned some time before the destruction of Pompeii.
The monument had seven Doric columns along its shorter sides and eleven along the longer ones. At the foot of the steps leading up to the temple there is a tomb-like structure which was probably a monument erected to the cult of the founder of the town. In front of the remains of the temple there are three pre-Roman tuff-stone altars and a well surrounded by a circular building with Doric columns, while at the rear we find a semicircular tuff-stone seat which enjoys an uninterrupted view of the Gulf of Naples.

The sacred area (possibly no more than a sacellum after the temple was abandoned) was used for athletic games, displays and also as a space for the public during the intervals of theatrical performances.

View of the base of the Doric temple.

Reconstruction of the Triangular Forum.

48 The Large Theatre

Although it is actually the only theatre in Pompeii it was given this name to distinguish it from the nearby Odeion. It was built in the 2nd century B.C according to traditional Greek canons in so far as the tiered seating makes use of a natural slope and the orchestra is arranged in a horse-shoe shape. It was extended and restored during the reign of Augustus at the personal expense of the Holconius brothers, who were rich Pompeiian vine growers.

The upper circle was added to increase the seating capacity and the two side boxes built above the entrances to the orchestra were reserved for the guests of honour.

The theatre of Pompeii could accommodate 5,000 people seated in three different areas which were separated by corridors. The first (called the *ima cavea*) was situated in the orchestra itself and had four rows of seats which were reserved for the decurions, while the first rows of the *media cavea* were for the representatives of the corporations: one of these was reserved for the eldest of the Holconius brothers and was identified by an inscription in bronze letters.The top part (*summa cavea*) was designated for the ordinary townspeople.

The final tier had stone rings fitted into the walls which were used to support the poles which held the large canopy covering the theatre to protect the audience from the sun.

The stone stage was rebuilt after the earthquake of 62 A.D. in imitation of the facade of an important building decorated with columns, niches and statues.

Layout of the Theatres and the Triangular Forum

1	Temple of Isis	4	Doric Temple	7	Large Theatre
2	Samnite Gymnasium	5	Tholos	8	Odeion
3	Triangular Forum	6	Gladiators' Barracks	9	Temple of Jupiter M.

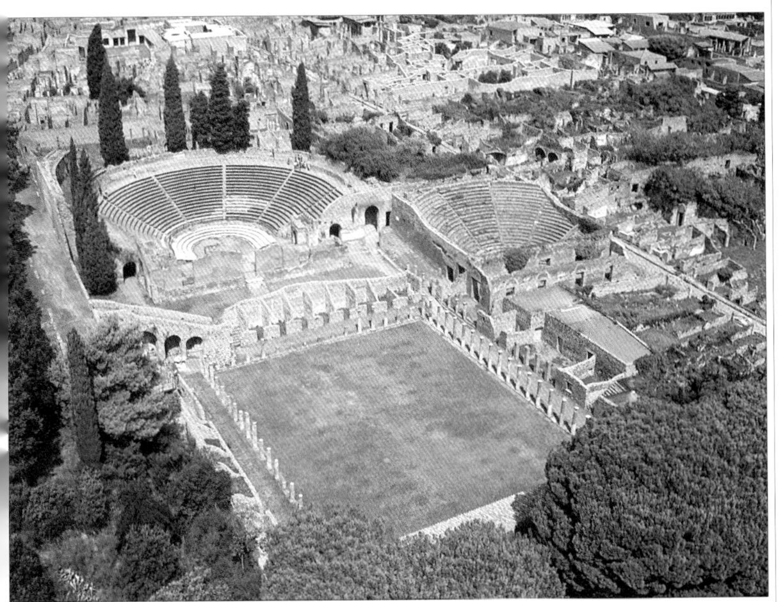

Aerial view of the Theatres.

49 THE GLADIATORS BARRACKS

In the latter years of Pompeii the four-sided colonnade rising up behind the Theatre was used as the barracks of the organisation of gladiators who performed in the town.
Along the wings of the colonnade and on the first floor were the rooms which provided accommodation for the gladiators from other towns. Paraments, helmets and arms were found in many of the rooms.
The four-sided colonnade was originally used as an extension of the theatre: for example, the public could go there for something to eat (performances often lasted most of the day) or to take shelter from the rain.
It is likely that for a few years this space was used both by the theatre and as the headquarters of an organisation responsible for the sporting, intellectual and military training of the town's youth.

The large courtyard of the Gladiators' Barracks.

50 THE ODEION

It was built by the same two duumviri responsible for the construction of the Amphitheatre during the early years of the Roman colony.
The tiered seating was cut away to one side to allow the construction of a perimeter wall designed to support the four-sided roof.
The first seats in front of the orchestra hemicycle, which was paved with slabs of coloured marble chips, were reserved for the decurions and were laid out on top of four rows of wide tuff-stone steps. The tiered seating was served by semicircular steps to the sides of the orchestra.
Boxes for the guests of honour were situated on either side of the stage area from which they could be reached, while three doors in the stage wall opened onto the backstage dressing room and from here led directly outside.

Imaginary reconstruction of the Odeion.

On the top of the tiered seating there are two unusual tuff-stone figures of telamons in a kneeling position and holding a shelf with decorative elements.

This covered theatre, used for concerts and for poetry recital, is situated near the Large Theatre.

51 THE TEMPLE OF JUPITER MEILICHIOS

The name of the temple was discovered thanks to an inscription in the Oscan language found on the Porta di Stabia gate. This cult enjoyed a particular following in Pompeii due to trade links with Magna Grecia, where it was fairly widespread.

The temple itself stands on a tall podium with four Corinthian columns at the front and two at the sides, behind which was the cella where terracotta statues of Jupiter and Juno and a bust of Minerva were found.

The discovery of the divinities of the Capitoline triad, who were worshipped in the *Capitolium* in the Forum, suggests that the cult had been temporarily transferred here after the earthquake of 62 A.D. while restoration work was being carried out on the main temple.

A Nucerian tuff-stone altar stands in the courtyard and dates back to between the 3rd and 2nd centuries B.C..

Imaginary reconstruction of the Temple of Jupiter Meilichios.

A statue of Jupiter Meilichios on display at the Archaelogical Museum in Naples. The name "meilichios" given to Jupiter - to whom this temple in Via Stabiana (near the Odeion) is dedicated - literally means "sweet as honey".

52 THE PORTA DI STABIA GATE

Located below the area where the theatres are to be found, this gate is held to be the oldest preserved at Pompeii. It must have been a particularly busy gateway to the city-deep ruts can be seen which would have been left by carriage wheels passing over the stone surface.

53 THE HOUSE OF THE CEII

This small house stands opposite the well-known House of Menander in Vicolo Meridionale, which can be reached directly from Via Stabiana by taking the side street almost opposite the Temple of Jupiter Meilichios.

The name was given to the house by the archaeologists who chose it from one of the nine election slogans painted on the front wall. The rooms are decorated with original third style paintings: in the winter *triclinium*, to the right of the four-columned *atrium* with its fountain in the *impluvium*, we see a young Bacchus offering wine to a tiger.The decorations on the three walls of the garden are particularly striking. They depict landscapes with pseudo-Egyptian motifs and scenes of wild beasts hunting: wolves chasing wild boars, a tiger chasing two rams and a lion pursuing a bull. There is also a Nile landscape depicting pygmies struggling with a hippopotamus and a crocodile.

The tetrastyle atrium of the house of Ceii.

A detail from the hunting scene painted on the front wall of the garden.

54 THE HOUSE OF MENANDER

The house belonged to Quintus Poppaeus, one of the Poppaeus family to whom Nero's second wife, Poppaea Sabina, most probably belonged. It extends over 2,000 square metres and reflects the traditional layout of a Roman house, with its *atrium* and *peristyle* as well as servants quarters and a bath-house.

Before admiring the large *peristyle* it is worth stopping briefly in the *atrium*, where the *lararium* is situated in the right-hand corner, and in the room to the left (opposite the *implu-vium*) where the walls are frescoed with a triptych inspired by the Trojan war. On the right we can see the death of Laocoon who, along with

The name derives from the fresco of the poet Menander, discovered in a room behind the peristyle.

Cassandra resisting abduction by Odysseus, one of the paintings from the triptych inspired by the Trojan war.

his children, was strangled by a snake; to the right, Cassandra resists abduction by Odysseus and lastly, in the centre, Cassandra tries to convince the Trojans not to let the wooden horse enter the city.

The floor of the living room in the *peristyle* in the right-hand corner just past the *tablinum* is of particular interest as it contains a charming mosaic in the centre depicting a scene with pygmies rowing a boat on the river Nile. On the walls decorated with a fourth style green background there are also scenes of Centaurs abducting the Lapithae women). A corridor opening to the right of the *peristyle* leads to the kitchens, several basement areas and the vegetable garden. In this area a box was discovered containing 118 items of silverware, some gold objects and a few coins, all of which had been stored away until restoration work on the house was completed. On returning to the *peristyle* we find the bath-house whose *calidarium* still has its original mosaic floor and painted stucco wall decorations.

Hunting scenes from the peristyle.

There are four niches at the rear of the *peristyle*, two of which are rectangular while the others are apsidal. The first one on the right is decorated with second style paintings and has an altar dedicated to the cult of the *Lares*, which were originally represented by five wooden or wax sculptures from which the plaster casts seen here were made.

Next to an apsidal niche there is a rectangular one with an illustration on the right-hand wall of the poet Menander seated.

Just before the corner of the *peristyle* there is a *cubiculum* which was originally a double bedroom. Beyond this area we find the part of the house where the servants lived and worked, with cells for

The atrium of the house.

the slaves, storerooms for wine and stables. After the main *peristyle* there is a large *triclinium* where some of the walls of the previous construction have been dug up. In the living room which opens out on the right we find the plaster casts of the bodies of twelve treasure-hunting thieves who had come here following the catastrophe of 79 A.D. with the intention of stripping the house of its valuable objects.

Altar with the plaster casts of the wooden or wax statues of the Lares.

Calidarium in the house's thermal baths.

THE FOUNTAINS

The town of Pompeii contained a wealth of public fountains.
The pictures illustrate a sequence of highly original subjects whose decorations were carved from blocks of marble or lava stone.

55 VIA DELL'ABBONDANZA

This street was the main artery of the city and connected the Porta Sarno gate with the Forum.
A fountain which represents the goddess of Fortune with her horn of plenty gave this street its name.
Numerous small shops and *termopoli* open out onto this main road, giving us a clear picture of its commercial nature.
After the 62 A.D. earthquake the centre of local economic life moved to the crossroads between via di Stabia and via dell'Abbondanza.

The fountain after which the "Via dell'Abbondanza" (Street of Plenty) is named.

56 THE HOUSE OF THE LYRE-PLAYER

This extremely large building (approximately 2,700 square metres) was created by joining together two residential complexes which covered an area nearly equal to that of the whole *insula*. The house can be entered both from Via dell'Abbondanza and from Via Stabiana. The house is arranged around two *atria* and three *peristyles*. Its name derives from a bronze statue of "Apollo playing the lyre" that is today housed in the Nat.Archaeological Museum in Naples with other magnificent paintings and bronze portraits of famous personalities, such as Marcellus, the nephew of Augustus and patron of Pompeii. As is inferred from electoral propaganda and a number of examples of graffiti, it belonged to the Popidius family.

The Statue of Apollo playing the lyre.

57 THE LAUNDRY OF STEPHANUS

This is the only building in Pompeii which was originally built as a laundry and fuller's workshop; the three other establishments of this kind were restructured residential buildings.
The fuller's workshop provided services to numerous clothiers, wool makers and tailors working in the town.
According to the electoral slogans painted on the facade (*"the united fullers recommend... Stephanus recommends"*), the establishment has been attributed to a certain *Stephanus*.
A press used to fold cloth was placed against the left wall of the large

The laundry of Stephanus.
Cloth was washed in the impluvium in the atrium.

entrance hall. Once past the entrance hall, we enter an *atrium* with a flat roof which served as a terrace to hang out the washing. Finer cloth was washed in the large parapeted tank in the middle of the atrium.
The *peristyle* at the rear of the atrium has three intercommunicating stone tubs and, alongside these, five basins where cloth was trodden by foot. A number of vessels containing urine were found nearby.
Urine was used to treat the cloth and was collected in terracotta amphorae which were stored in separate rooms not far from the workshop itself. The kitchen and a lavatory are reached through a door in the left-hand corner of the *peristyle*.

**The laundry of Stephanus.
A tub for bleaching cloth in urine.**

58 Workshop of Verecundus

Returning to and crossing Via dell'Abbondanza, we reach the entrance to a shop in which activities linked to those of the laundry were carried out. This is the so-called "Workshop of Verecundus", which was a felting establishment. As with many buildings in this street, only the facade now remains. The plaster on the facade is covered with illustrated advertisements showing the manufacturing phases of the articles that were made in it, among which felt shoes and ready-made clothes which were sold directly to the public.

A detail of the painted facade of the Workshop of Verecundus.

The town's economic life

A WORKING TOWN

Many of the town's inhabitants were farmers, but the town's excellent geographic position with respect to the villages further inland and the location of a river port not far from the sea also gave great impetus to trade closely connected to agricultural produce. Several kinds of arts and crafts also played an important role in the local economy. Some workshops were engaged in the whole wool manufacturing process from shearing to tailoring, while the washing and dying process was performed in the fullers' workshops.

To bleach cloth the fullers used human urine which was collected directly from Pompeiian households where it was stored in "portable" containers placed alongside the streets.

Other workshops produced the famous fish sauce called *garum*, while bread was made in over thirty bakeries with annexed mills.

Of course there was also a wealth of pottery-makers and ceramists, blacksmiths, joiners and carpenters, marble-carvers, goldsmiths and *scriptores*, i.e. artisans whose job it was to paint red and black election slogans and other notices to the public, most of which are still visible on the walls.

The wealthiest and most powerful corporation of artisans in the town was that of the wool-makers and clothiers in general, as is confirmed by the imposing building in the Forum which they dedicated to the patron of their trade, the priestess Eumachia.

As the town was a flourishing trading centre, thousands of people would flock towards it every day from the surrounding areas. The *hospitia* (boarding houses) in which they found accommodation were either annexed to the *cauponae* (taverns) and *thermopolia*, where they could have a warm meal as in our modern-day "fast-food restaurants", or to the *tabernae*, which served the excellent wine from the vineyards on the slopes of Mount Vesuvius.

Numerous, mostly one-room shops ran all along the main streets and all kinds of articles were on sale on masonry counters. Almost every family - even the relatively wealthy ones - used to rent out rooms to passing tradesmen since it was an easy source of income. In many cases the owners were also directly in charge of sales, as is witnessed by the passageways between the residential areas of the houses and the shops.

Sign from Euxinus' Inn with the greeting "Be as happy as the Phoenix".

Fullers at work. A painting associated with the cloth trade.

59 THE THERMOPOLIUM (I 8,8)

Walking further down Via dell'Abbondanza in the direction of the Porta di Sarno Gate, we reach Pompeii's equivalent of a "fast-food" restaurant, where warm meals could be bought and eaten on the spot.
Coins for a total weight of about 3 kg, equivalent in worth to about 680 *sesterces*, were found in one of the wall recesses.
Given the large quantity of change (374 *asses* and 1,237 *quadrantes*, each worth one quarter of an as), these were probably the takings of a single day's business.
The shop is completed by a sacellum dedicated to Mercury and Dionysus and a small shrine for the tutelary deities of the household.
The publican's own apartment extended to the rear of the shop and was reached through an independent entrance door which opened onto a narrow side street.
A magnificent specimen of late 3rd - style decoration can be seen in the *triclinium*.

The "*thermopolion*" on Via dell'Abbondanza is an example of an ancient "fast-food" restaurant. Warm cooked foods were stored in a masonry counter and were eaten on the spot.

60 ASELLINA'S TAVERN

Behind the facade of the tavern, which borders on Via dell'Abbondanza and is covered all over with election propaganda, we can see a masonry counter which contained four terra-cotta vessels for storing cooked meals.
At the rear of the tavern are the remains of the staircase which led to the guest rooms on the upper floor. The graffiti on the walls of these rooms suggest that customers could also enjoy the company of Asellina's waitresses.

The tavern-keeper Asellina as well as Zmyrina, Ismurna and Aegle were influential women who used to sign electoral propaganda to support candidates in the elections for high municipal offices.

The entrance door to Asellina's Tavern and the painted sign still visible on the facade.

61 House of the Floral Bed Chambers

The entrance to this house is blocked by a plaster mould of the wooden door knockers, and for this reason it can only be entered from the shop adjacent. Particularly interesting are the third-style pictures which can be found in three different places. Two of these are of clear Egyptian inspiration. The pale background, typical of the final phase of the third style, works to great effect here.

62 House of Paquius Proculus

In this house, which belonged to a well-known personality in ancient Pompeii, sacrifices dedicated to the goddess Venus were carried out, as can be seen from the domestic altar decorated with images of lovebirds. This Samnite-type house has an atrium with a mosaic floor which depicts a guard dog.
The decorations of the entire house were particularly rich.

Portrait of Paquius Proculus and his wife.

House of the floral bed chambers. Detail of the fruit garden painted on the walls of the black cubiculum.

The mosaic shows the projection of the entrance hall with a guard dog.

63 HOUSE OF THE CRYPTOPORTICUS

This house takes the name of *cryptoporticus*, or "covered gallery", and formerly belonged to the house next to the Sacellum Iliacus. The rooms of the *cryptoporticus* contain some magnificent pictures, dating from the first century B.C.. The house seems to be in a particularly poor state seeing as at the moment of the eruption in 79 A.D. restoration work to repair the serious damage to the building done by the 62 A.D. earthquake had just begun.

Wall decoration of the covered gallery. On the frieze above the frame there were fifty pinax (small square frames) which depicted episodes from Homer's Iliad.

64 THE HOUSE OF THE EPHEBE

This residential complex is situated in a side street of Via dell'Abbondanza, not far from the House of Menander, and actually comprises three buildings converted into one.
It derives its name from the bronze statue of an Ephebe which was found in the house and was used to support oil-lamps needed to light the *triclinium* couches during evening receptions. Access to the house was through the second entrance-door and the *Tuscan atrium* which was flanked to the right by the family's living quarters and, on the left, by the reception rooms and areas devoted to leisure activities and sport. Here, in addition to a few living-rooms, we find a large open *triclinium* which was once surrounded by a shaded garden with a fountain whose jets were forced through walls decorated with several wild animals and Nile landscapes.
A larger *triclinium* is situated has an extraordinary mosaic floor made from valuable marble and glass paste tiles which form a magnificent composition of flowers set within a fantastic scene of buildings depicted in perspective.

The House of the Ephebe. The summer triclinium.

65 House of the Chaste Lovers

This house included a bakers, with four millstones for the grain as well as an oven. The residential part has a number of fourth-style pictures and, in the *triclinium*, elegant third-style decoration, amongst which can be found a small picture showing the "chaste lovers".

A room in the House of the Chaste Lovers.
Below: picture showing a banquet.

66 House of Amandus the Priest

The rooms of this house, which line the road, were detached from one another and adapted for use as shops with storerooms. On a fragment of a painting on the wall in the entrance of this house the name *Spartacs* can be read, written in the Oscan language, above one of the mounted warriors.

The *triclinium* contains pictures in the third style with four large pictures at the centre of the walls; in one of these the fall of Icarus after going too close to the rays of the sun is depicted.

Spartacus on Mount Vesuvius

In 71 B.C. there was a slaves' revolt in the school for gladiators in Capua. This revolt was led by Spartacus.
Around a year later, the original rebels were joined by other slaves escaping inhuman conditions in all parts of the country. Spartacus found a refuge on the slopes of Mount Vesuvius, on the inhospitable mountain. The Roman Consul Clodius Gabrus brought his legions to the foot of the volcano and was unexpectedly defeated by the rebels' surprise manoeuvre. The victorious Spartacus and his allies settled themselves in, terrorising the inhabitants of the local towns - one of which was Pompeii.
The rebellion was only quelled two years later, when the Consul Crassus brought down an entire army made up of 60,000 men ready for anything. The few survivors came to a bad end.

67 HOUSE OF IULIUS POLYBIUS

Numerous electoral posters indicate that Iulius Polybius, descendent of a family of freed slaves, was the last inhabitant of this dwelling. He encouraged people to vote for his election as *duumvir* by guaranteeing "good bread". The house, from the second century B.C., is organised in a different way to the typical Pompeiian house. Proceeding inwards from the entrance, we do not arrive at the *atrium*, but instead in a rectangular room which includes one of the finest examples of first-style painting.

Venus regarding herself in a mirror, aided by a cupid.

68 HOUSE OF TREBIUS VALENS

The proprietor of this house, a tile maker, descended from an ancient Samnite family.

A piece of graffiti found in a cubiculum informs us that Ura (almost certainly a slave) gave birth on Thursday January 23rd; in another the message "*Valens, if I was your woman...*" can be read.

Open triclinium. The remains of four people looking for shelter from the hail of rocks and died when the roof collapsed were found in one corner of the peristyle.

69 THE BAKERY OF SOTERICUS

Some of the excellent bread for which the area around Vesuvius was renowned was made in this bakery on Via dell'Abbondanza opposite the House of Trebius Valens. As the building did not include a shop, the bread produced was evidently sold elsewhere. This was one of the thirty-one bakeries and cake shops in the town and the name of its reputed owner, *Sotericus*, appears on the front of the inn next-door. The large workshop where bread was made extended across two older buildings and was equipped with shelves, worktops and a dough kneading machine. The workshop also had an oven, a grain warehouse, a bedroom for the workers and four different-size machines driven by donkeys.

70 SCHOLA ARMATURARUM (Military School)

Trophies and palm fronds are painted on the entrance to this large room which indicate the military nature of the association which had its headquarters here. Numerous weapons were found in this building, all stored on wooden shelves, imprints from which can still be seen on the walls.

Reconstruction of the façade of the Schola Armaturarum.

71 HOUSE OF THE MORALIST

This house belonged to Epidius Hymenaeus, a wine merchant. From the seal of Arrius Crescens discovered inside, it is now thought that this latter person lived in the connecting house, at number 2. "*Do not look lasciviously at the woman of another, nor make comely eyes at her, and do not use bad language*" - this is one of the three inscriptions found on the walls of the summer triclinium, all of which encourage sober behaviour.

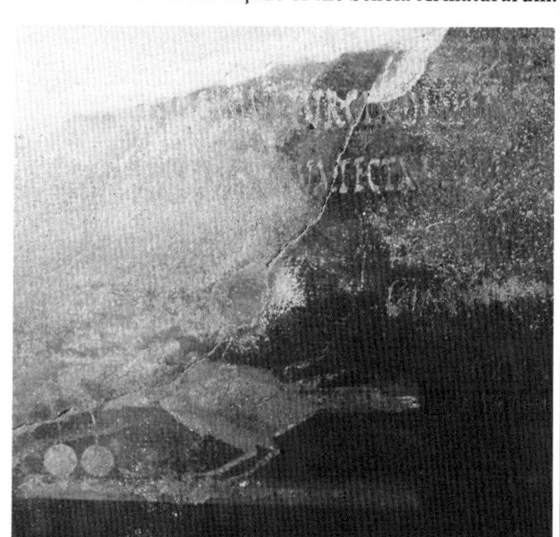

Summer triclinium. Above: detail of inscriptions on the walls.

72 HOUSE OF PINARIUS CERIALIS

The owner of this house was a priest of the cult of Hercules, as can be deduced from the sacrificial knife found in the house and by the words "drinker of pure wine" found written in the house.
The jeweller Pinarius Cerialis worked with and traded in precious stones and cameos - a box containing 114 gems and a number of instruments was found here.

Particularly interesting are the magnificent fourth-style theatrical decorations, which can be seen in a cubiculum, and which are inspired by Euripide's tragedy Iphigenia in Tauris.

73 House of D. Octavius Quartius

This complex stretches across nearly the whole area of the insula which is bounded on one side by Via dell'Abbondanza and, on the other, by the outer wall of the Large Palaestra in the Amphitheatre area.

The residential section of this complex is a particularly luxurious building which, although not exceptionally big, boasts the largest garden in Pompeii.

The garden has recently been restored and planted with the species of trees which are thought to have originally been grown in it.

The house has a large *atrium* with numerous bed chambers (*cubicula*) arranged all round it and its impluvium is surrounded by a low masonry flower bed. The *cubiculum* which is reached by turning left from the entrance hall contains a stove for baking terracotta pots.

A bronze seal found near the stove suggests the house belonged to a certain D. Octavius Quartius, whilst until recently the numerous election slogans painted on its external walls had led archaeologists to assume that it was the property of Loreius Tiburtinus.

The room in the bottom left-hand corner was originally a living-room and was later changed into a passage leading to the lavatory and kitchen at the rear of the house.

The portrait of Loreius Tiburtinus dressed as a high-priest of Isis.

Walking across the *atrium* we enter a small square *peristyle* surrounded by a number of rooms, of which the most remarkable is a large reception hall.

The lower half of the walls has an imitation marble decoration bordered by two friezes: the lower one portrays the feats of the Greeks at Troy and the upper one illustrates the expedition of Hercules against Laomedon. One section of the T-shaped water channel in the back garden extends along the width of the building while the second section runs from one end of the garden to the other.

On the right of the first section of the water channel is a room with fourth-style decorations including the image of a high-priest of Isis, suggesting that the room was used as a sacellum for the cult of this goddess. Opposite it, alongside an apsidal fountain, is a *biclinium* which was used when the family dined in the open air.

The frescoes on the bottom walls of the *biclinium* portray Narcissus at the Fountain (on the right) and Pyramus and Thisbe, the two lovers who committed suicide, (on the left).

At the junction of the two water channels is a four-columned aedicula containing a nymphaeum which supplied water to the more than 50-metre-long channel. Originally the garden area was entirely covered with pergolas and enclosed all round by high-trees and was used for the nocturnal rites in honour of the goddess Isis.

It is assumed that the two sections of the water channel could be made to flood the whole area in order to imitate the Nile floods to which the fertility of the Egyptian fields was owed.

Narcissus at the fountain.

Pyramus and Thisbe.

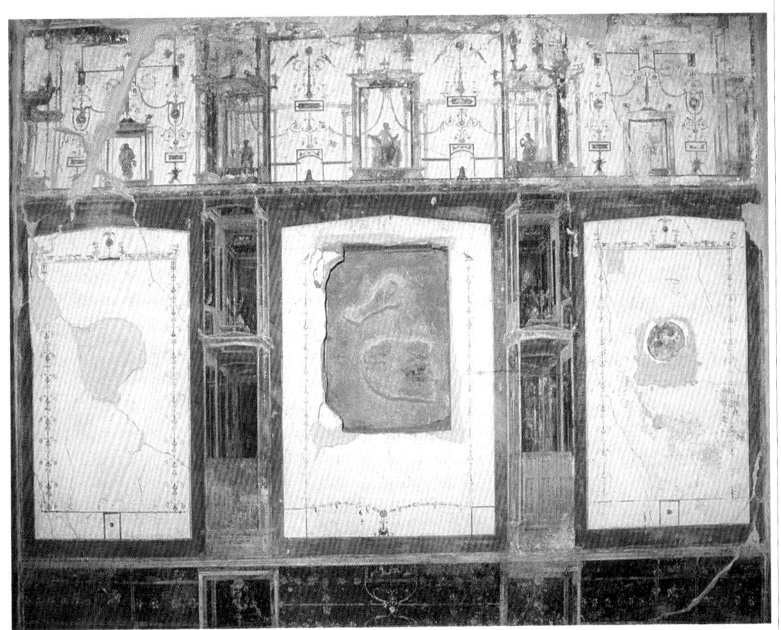

The paintings in the sacellum dedicated to the goddess Isis.

A view of the water channel running through the garden of the house.

74 THE HOUSE OF VENUS

The focal point of this house is the *peristyle*, which is sumptuously decorated with painted garden features (fountains, hedges, birds, flowers, sculptures). On the rear wall there is a painting that portrays a naked Venus with a head of curly hair and resplendent with gold jewels, sailing in a shell with billowing sails accompanied by a retinue of cupids. From an artistic point of view, the painting is of poor quality, but its colours are well arranged and the overall effect is highly dramatic.

Panel with a view of the sea.

The large fresco of "Venus in the shell".

The peristyle and the garden..

75 THE HOUSE OF JULIA FELIX

Thanks to its large size and particular typology, this house can be defined a "villa". It extends over an area corresponding to two *insulae*, of which one-third is occupied by the building proper and two-thirds were used as a vegetable garden.

After the earthquake of 62 A.D., the owner of this sumptuous and elegant house, Julia Felix, daughter of Spurius, decided to ease the difficulties caused by the shortage of accommodation by renting out part of the house. As the Forum Baths could be used only in part, she also opened her private baths to the public. The notice painted on the facade reads "*elegant bathing facilities, shops with annexed apartments upstairs and independent apartments on the first floor are offered for rent to respectable people*". Also the maximum lease term, a period of five years "*from August 1st next to August 1st of the sixth year*", is specified.

The house was divided into three parts. The baths, with access from Via dell'Abbondanza, were provided with all the required facilities and an open swimming-pool. The owner's apartment looks out onto a magnificent garden with a water channel surrounded on all sides by original marble-embellished quadrangular columns. Lastly there were the shops, some of which opened onto Via dell'Abbondanza and some onto the side-street leading to the Large Palaestra. The rented lodgings were also situated on this side-street.

The sculptures which decorated the garden and some of the paintings found in the house are now on show at the National Archaeological Museum in Naples, while a fresco with Apollo and the Muses is exhibited in the Louvre, Paris.

The original colonnades of the House of Julia Felix, which was first discovered in 1755.

Eating habits

Vegetables and Garum Sauce

Finds of charred foodstuffs informed us of what the Pompeiians used to eat. Vegetables and fruit were basic components of the Pompeiian diet, along with bread. Vegetables were also grown in kitchen gardens and their abundant use in cooking confirms the nickname of "herb eaters" given to the Romans by Plautus. Pliny the Elder classified about one thousand edible plants, many of which were highly praised for their therapeutic properties.

A famous type of cabbage grown in the area was well known and highly appreciated in Rome under the name of Pompeii cabbage or "cauliflower". In "*De Agricultura*" Cato praised it as the "supreme vegetable".

"If, during a banquet, you intend to drink a lot and eat with appetite - Cato suggests - *have some raw cauliflower before and after your meal and you will feel as if you had not eaten anything at all and you can drink as much as you like*".

Several kinds of lettuce very similar to those still in use today were grown in the countryside around Pompeii as well as endivcs, flowering broccoli, basil, carrots, cress and leeks. In addition to onions and garlic, which the poorer classes used not only to season all sorts of dishes but also as their main dish, leeks were classed by Pliny as first-class vegetables.

Charred remains of melon seeds, broad beans, peas, chick-peas and lentils provide precise information on what was produced and thus eaten in Pompeii.

Olives were also a favourite in Pompeii; they were grown throughout the countryside and were either pickled in vinegar or salt or used to make oil.

Various everyday lifestyles in Pompeii are documented by finds of household articles and by "pictures" painted on the walls in numerous rooms. Indeed paintings were used not only for decoration but also as "catalogues" of family habits and tastes as well as to illustrate the social status of the owner.

Remains of walnuts, chestnuts and almonds have also been found in some houses, where they were stored on shelves as provisions available for family use.

Several kinds of fresh fruit were on sale in the well-stocked town market, including apples, pomegranates, quinces, pears, grapes, figs and plums. In the years immediately before the eruption fruit trees imported from abroad such as cherry, apricot and peach trees had become more and more common. The inhabitants of Pompeii adopted sophisticated procedures to preserve vegetables and fruit. Vegetables for the winter were put in vinegar or brine, while fruit was dried and then preserved in honey, which was also used in large quantities mixed with wine.

Well-known cheeses (*caseus*) and smoked cheeses, were also made from sheep's or cow's milk.

The Pompeiians used to dress their dishes with a sauce, called *garum*, which was prepared by soaking several kinds of ungutted blue-fish, such as tuna, in brine.

Garum was so popular throughout Pompeii that there were several workshops which produced and sold different blends of this sauce.

Examples of these are wicker-baskets full of fresh ricotta cheese, pots filled with the special vegetables grown in kitchen gardens around the town, for instance leek and cauliflower; bowls containing several kinds of fruit such as grapes, figs, chestnuts, apples and pomegranates and compositions depicting poultry and geese, fish and shellfish.

76 The Necropolis outside the Porta Nocera Gate

A wealth of tombs have been unearthed just outside the Porta Nocera gate. A monumental exedra-shaped tomb is dedicated to *Eumachia*, the priestess of the cult of Venus and to whom a building in the Forum is dedicated. Further on is the *Tomb of the Flavius family*: 8 of its niches are situated over the door and some of the 6 niches on either side are decorated with tuff-stone busts and inscriptions.

Some of the most interesting of these are high-podium tombs such as the one of *Publius Vesonius Phileros* or the four-niched tomb of *Marcus Octavius.* The former is of particular interest because of its length inscription in the middle of the podium. Complaining of having been unjustly accused by a friend, Vesonius addresses passers-by with the words: "*If it is not too much of an inconvenience, stop here for a moment and learn about the dangers you should be wary of. The man whose name is mentioned below and who* - so I thought - *was my friend brought false charges against me. Through the intervention of the gods and thanks to my innocence I was acquitted of every charge in court. My hope is that the person who has slandered me will be rejected by the gods of the household and those of the afterworld*".

A wealth of tombs which formed the town's necropolis have been unearthed along a 250-metre stretch of the road running along the town walls just outside the Porta Nocera gate.

Titus Suedius Clemens

Repairing the damage wrought by the earthquake in 62 A.D. caused an enormous drain on resources, seeing as it involved most of the city.

These great reconstruction works could not be described as a "clean" operation, seeing as the Emperor Vespasian was forced to send his Tribune Titus Suedius Clemens down to Pompeii. The Tribune was given special powers to resolve problems relating to illegal building on public space and other various controversies caused by the confusion. It was only with his intervention that the colony managed to preserve its architectural heritage. The Roman Prefect's orders were all posted around the gates of the city.

77 THE GARDEN OF THE FUGITIVES

The name given to this rural dwelling reflects the dramatic events that took place in its large vegetable garden. More than any other, the scene which unfolds in the "Garden of the Fugitives" revives the full horror of the tragic death suffered by the inhabitants of Pompeii during the eruption of Vesuvius in 79 A.D.. We can see the plaster casts of the bodies of thirteen people, among them whole families of young people with their children, who met their death while trying to save their lives by fleeing towards the town gates in the direction of the sea.

The bodies of eleven other victims, including a pregnant woman, have recently been found not far from the Garden of the Fugitives.

78 THE AMPHITHEATRE

The term amphitheatre is literally defined as "the space for the spectators that runs all round the arena". The commemorative inscription attributes its construction to the highest officials in Pompeii, Caius Quintus Valgus and Marcus Portius, who also built the Odeion shortly after the town had acquired the status of a Roman colony.

The Pompeiian Amphitheatre is classed as the oldest of all existing buildings of this kind.

About 20,000 people could be seated in its three tiers and would attend bloody shows performed by gladiators and wild animals.

No shows were held in the amphitheatre in the winter months and in the warmest period of the year. In summer, a canopy of dark flax material was fitted above the seats to protect the audience from the burning sun and this was advertised in the notices announcing the shows. The canopy was supported on wooden poles inserted into stone rings fixed to the walls on the upper landings of the stairways.

A number of external stairways led to the upper tiers (*summa cavea*) which formed the top part of the structure. From a passageway running parallel to the perimeter of the arena, and from here over several stairways, the spectators could reach the middle and lower tiers (*ima cavea* and *media cavea*). Carts would enter the amphitheatre through two corridors which led to the slightly flattened ends of the arena directly from outside. The wild animals used for the shows entered the arena through a narrow passage in the middle of the arena.

During the gladiatorial games in 59 A.D. a violent brawl broke out between spectators from Pompeii and others from the nearby town of Nuceria and many people were killed or wounded; the people from Nuceria came off worse and this unprecedented incident was discussed in the Roman Senate at the request of Nero. The Pompeiian Amphitheatre was closed for ten years and all the "supporters" organizations were disbanded. Through the intercession of Nero's second wife Poppaea the period of "disqualification" was subsequently shortened and the Amphitheatre resumed its activity after 62 A.D..

79 THE LARGE PALAESTRA

The Palaestra was the largest of all the public spaces, the sports activities performed in it were intended to serve to inculcate the Imperial ideology in the minds of the younger generations. In compliance with a decree issued by the Emperor, the town's youths were organized into associations called "*collegia iuvenum*". The palaestra measures 141 metres by 107 metres and is surrounded by a high wall with ten entrance gates. On three sides it is enclosed by colonnades of 48 columns on the longer side and 35 columns on each of the shorter sides.

A swimming-pool measuring 35 metres by 22 metres situated right in the middle of the palaestra.

80 THE HOUSE OF FABIUS RUFUS

This is one of the so-called "town villas" which was built against the town walls in the last period of the town's life. The villa had a fine view over the Gulf of Naples and its interior was entirely decorated in the Pompeiian fourth style.

The villa itself is the result of the fusion of a number of previously built houses and so, in a tiny room in the central apsidal structure, we can find the remains of second style frescoes, including what appears to be a portrait of the Venus of Pompeii. The side walls in the same area are also decorated with stars and small moon designs, suggesting that the room may have been used for astrology.

A second style fresco portraying the Venus of Pompeii.

A theatrical mask.

A living room decorated with fourth-style frescoes.

81 THE HOUSE OF SALLUST

This house, which is situated in the town's western quarter just before the street forks to the left towards the Porta Erco-lano gate, is one of the oldest in Pompeii, dating from the 3rd century B.C.. In addition to the atrium with its surrounding rooms, it has a small covered porch behind the tablinum, a garden and a summer triclinium with stone couches. Towards the rear of the building there is a kitchen, a dining room and several bedrooms. The front of the building houses four shops, a tavern and a bakery with three millstones and an oven with a fireplace alongside. The owner probably took advantage of the house's proximity to the Porta Ercolano gate and converted it into a boarding house with a number of bedrooms on the first floor and a restaurant nextdoor.

The front of the House of Sallust.

The atrium of the house decorated with 1st style frescoes.

82 THE PORTA ERCOLANO GATE AND THE NECROPOLIS

This gate was certainly one of the most important in the town. All the carts and wagons coming from the harbour passed through the Porta Ercolano, as did all commercial traffic heading towards Naples. The gate was also known as the *Porta Salis*, the Gate of Salt, because it led to the "*Salinae Herculeae*" salt works which may have been situated on the coast near the mouth of the river Sarno. Beyond the Porta Ercolano gate on Via dei Sepolcri we find the tombs built between the founding of the colony (80 B.C.) and the destruction of the town. The commonest types of tombs were those with an aedicula, those with an exedra, and those surrounded by a wall or fence with an altar on a podium. However, we also find monumental funeral buildings with seats for the relatives of the dead, such as that of M. Cerrinus Restitutus.

Porta Ercolano Gate.

Tomb with altar belonging to Caius Calventius Quietus.

Tomb of Naevoleia Tyche. Relief panels.

From tomb 8, the "Blue Vase" in glass and cameo showing cupids making wine.

Imaginary reconstruction of Via dei Sepolcri.

83 THE VILLA OF DIOMEDES

This sumptuous villa was built just outside the Porta Ercolano gate in sight of the town walls.
An entrance on Via dei Sepolcri led straight into the 14-column *peristyle* around which the various rooms and !living quarters of the house were situated. The house's bath area was situated in a triangular space between the road and the *peristyle* while the *triclinium*/ living room opposite commanded a view over the Gulf of Naples and the large garden below. In the centre of the garden was an open-air *triclinium* and a swimming pool surrounded by a covered gallery (*cryptoporticus*).
Here the master of the house, with his 'treasure' of 1356 *sesterces*, and 18 other people, mainly heavily bejeweled wo-men, met their death as they tried to flee during the eruption. Their remains were found when the villa was excavated between 1771 and 1774.

Perystile with garden.

The cryptoporticus.

Reconstruction of the garden with a view of the Sorrentine peninsula and the isle of Capri.

84 THE HOUSE OF THE SURGEON

This is one of the oldest houses in Pompeii: it was built in the fourth century B.C. using local limestone from the river Sarno, which can still be seen in large blocks making up the façade. Forty medical instruments were found here, including gynaecological forceps, catheters and pliers for pulling out teeth.

MEDICINE IN POMPEII

Medicine was a scientia herbarum, a "herbal science", which mixed experience with popular beliefs. Medicinal preparations were based on herbs, roots or other commonly used elements such as honey, vinegar, bread, oil and wine. "*Laser*", an extract of the *laseripcium* root was used as a digestive, in circulatory disorders and was applied as a poultice to wounds; it was also believed that it could cure sore throat, asthma, jaundice and other infections. Pliny the Elder wrote that laserpicium was "*one of the greatest gifts that nature has given us*". Other widely-used vegetable substances were balsam, saffron, cumin, cinnamon, marjoram and poppyseeds. Often it was the patients themselves, or their families, who would take care of the preparation of medicines. Later, the medical profession became somewhat more widespread and thus the preparation of pharmaceutical substances became their duty. "Drug sellers" were also frequent - travelling salesmen who advertised products of dubious therapeutical quality.

Adonis wounded.

This became such a problem that in Rome in 81 B.C. the *Lex Cornelia* was issued to punish vendors of harmful medicines. Some prescriptions would have had a fair level of efficacy: there is the case of the disinfectant prepared by a Judean slave which is described by *Celsus* - "*two parts of calcium, one of sodium bicarbonate and child's urine*" - or the therapy for scabies based on tar and sulphur, again prescribed by Celsus. He also recommended the use of goose fat to treat inflammation of the uterus, and Pliny sustained that eating a snake was good for the health, swollen lymph nodes in particular. Medicines were presented in various forms: from packets of pills to herbal teas. The bile of vipers or lynxes was used to prepare eye drops. Poultices were applied to sick parts of the body, and were usually made up of dried vegetables ground into a flour then made into a paste by adding liquid and cooking until they had the consistency of a paste. Waxes were used in a similar way to poultices but instead used boiled beeswax, while other mixtures used mineral substances.

Pastels were prepared by powdering the ingredients and making a paste of them by adding vinegar or wine; a rubbery substance was then added and they were rolled out into small finger-like shapes and left to dry. The producer's seal was added to the final product along with instructions for dosage and use.

85 THE VILLA OF MYSTERIES

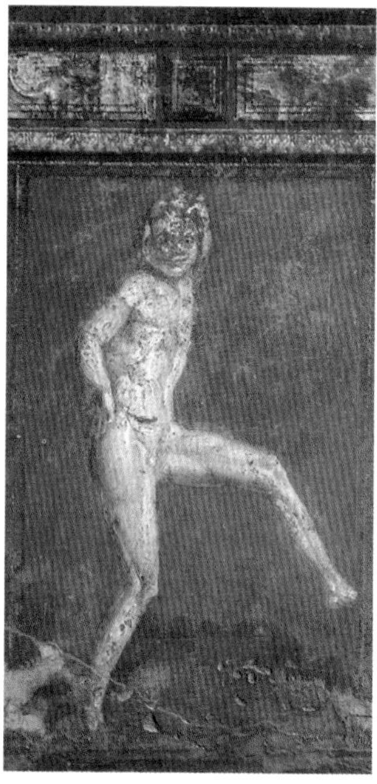

The villa owes its fame to the extraordinary wall paintings in the *triclinium* which make up an almost photographic sequence of theatrical scenes.
The building can be divided into two areas. The main area is exclusively residential and was built in the 2nd century B.C. with the sole purpose of providing a luxurious and comfortable place in which to live. The other part is linked to the villa's role as a working farm and hence was built with a view to accommodating the produce of the surrounding countryside.
It was added onto the former building in the 1st century A.D.

In the farm area on the right of the main entrance (1), archaeologists found the wine-press that was situated in the rooms where the wine was made (2). On the opposite side of the *peristyle* (3) are the kitchens, two ovens in the courtyard (4), the *lararium* and a large lavatory (5).
Beyond the kitchen courtyard we find a bath-house dating from the pre-Roman era which was subsequently used as store rooms (6). These open onto a small four-columned *atrium* (7) where we also find a number of smaller rooms decorated in the second style, including a *cubiculum* with two beds (double alcove) (8).

Outside view of the villa on the cryptoporticus. In the 1st century A.D. the better-off classes decided to change their way of living. The ancient and noble families now lived permanently in the country villas to get away from the chaos and new lifestyle of Pompeii, characterised by the political and cultural domination of the "uncultured" traders and businessmen.

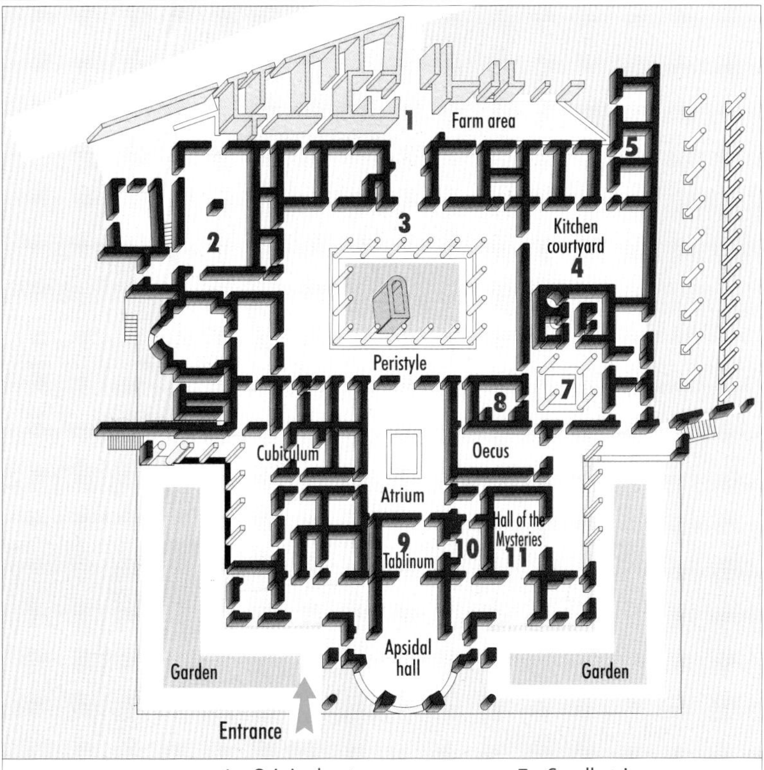

1 Farm area
5
3
2
Kitchen courtyard
4
Peristyle
7
8
Cubiculum
Oecus
Atrium
Hall of the Mysteries
9
Tablinum
10
11
Apsidal hall
Garden
Garden
Entrance

Plan of the Villa of Mysteries

1 Original entrance
2 Torcularium
3 Peristyle
4 Kitchen courtyard
5 Lavatory
6 Bathrooms no longer in use
7 Small atrium
8 Cubiculum
9 Tablinum
10 Cubiculum
11 'Hall of the Mysteries' (triclinium)

Imaginary reconstruction of the Villa of Mysteries.

The *tablinum* (9) is embellished with third style decorations on a black background depicting Egyptian figurines and miniaturised elements from the cult of Dionysus.
The *tablinum* leads into a *cubiculum* (10) whose original alcoves were made into doorways so as to convert the room into a corridor.
The imitation marble decoration is superimposed with panel pictures portraying sacrificial scenes and a fresco of Dionysus with a satyr and dancing maenads. These figures, along with the paintings of sculptures of a dancing satyr, the muse Calliope and Silenus with a hand-servant, set the scene for the nearby "*Triclinium of Mysteries*" (11).
The latter room, like almost all the residential part of the house, is situated on a three-sided *cryptoporticus* that had to be built because of the natural slope of the ground and so as to create a colonnade adjoining onto living rooms looking out onto the splendid view of the Gulf of Naples.

Tablinum (9).
Detail of a fresco showing Egyptian-style figures.

Below left: the wine-press (2); on the right: the peristyle (3).

Biclinium (10). Small picture showing the sacrifice of a pig to Priapus.

Oecus of the villa looking onto the side garden.
Below: architectural decoration in second style of a double alcove cubiculum.

The Painting of the Mysteries

The cycle of frescoes painted on the walls of the villa's panoramic dining room (11) draws its inspiration from a Greek work of the 4th or 3rd century B.C..

The "mystery" of the fresco (which is 17 metres long and 3 metres high) lies above all in its interpretation. However, the predominant theory is that the pictures making up the overall composition illustrate the various phases of the initiation of a young woman, perhaps a new bride, to the Dionysiac mysteries.

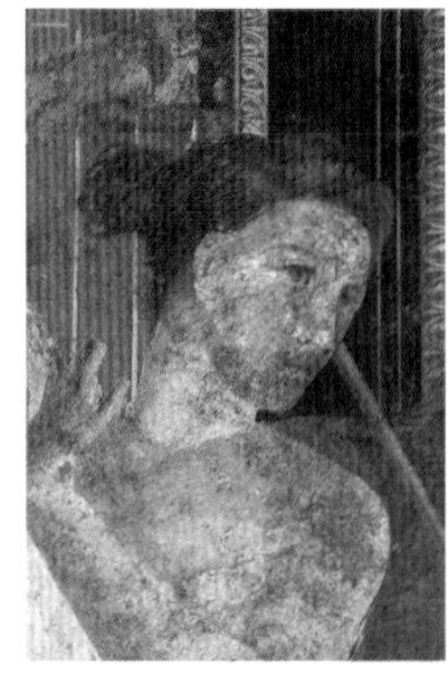

The orgiastic abandon which typifies the cult of Dionysus is here toned down and occasionally rendered through symbolic references but never with unbridled license. It must be remembered that the cult of Dionysus was not approved of by the Roman Senate, and harsh penalties were inflicted on initiates in an attempt, often to no avail, to limit or prevent the excesses to which they abandoned themselves during the "*Bacchanalia*".

I - Reading of the ritual and the initiate
II - Sacrifice and libation
III - Musician and pastoral scene
IV - Frightened woman

V - Silenus plies the satyrs with drink
VI - Dionysis and Arianne
VII - The Cista mistica with unveiled phallus and flagellant
VIII - Flagellated woman and follower of Bacchus

IX - Nuptial attire and Eros
X - "Domina"

Frieze of the Mysteries. List of interpretations of the various scenes.

The sequence of the fresco painting

Starting from the left-hand wall, we can see no less than 28 life-size figures depicted on a podium set against a red background; the section of the wall in which the door stands depicts a woman wearing a veil, who could be either **the matron of the household** or **a priestess**.
The **initiate** listens to a naked boy (perhaps **the youth Dionysus**) reading the precepts of the ritual under the watchful eye of the **matron** or **priestess**, with one hand on the boy's neck while in the other she holds a rolled parchment.
Next to her we see a **young girl** carrying a tray of offerings towards a **priestess** seated between two **hand-maidens** who are helping her to prepare the sacrifice.
Here the sequence seems to be interrupted by the figure of **Silenus** leaning on a column and playing the lyre, while a seated satyr (**Pan**) plays the pipes behind a **female panisc** suckling a goat at her breast. We are struck by the figure of **a woman** who is apparently disturbed by the following scenes and seems to be trying to run away, as is suggested by her billowing cape.
The sequence continues on the central wall, where we can see **Silenus seated** and offering a cup to a **satyr** while **another satyr** behind him holds up a tragic theatrical mask in an attempt to frighten him by causing its reflection to appear in the wine in the cup. Leaning back on the legs of **Ariadne** is the god **Dionysus**, perhaps inebriated or merely exhausted after the frenzy of the orgiastic ceremony. A kneeling woman, **the initiate**, holds out a hand to remove the veil covering the phallus, the symbol of Dionysus.
Next we see a **winged figure** flogging a **young woman**, who is painted on the right-hand wall, kneeling down and looking for protection in the lap of **another woman**.
The naked girl dancing in front of **another young woman** is a **Bacchante** seized by the orgiastic frenzy.
We then find another **bride** washing in preparation for her initiation to the mystery.
Finally, we see the matron of the household, a **priestess of Dionysus**, who probably commissioned the "mystery" to be painted on the walls of her villa.

3rd, 4th, 5th scenes of the huge fresco decorating the so-called "Hall of the Mysteries".

On the left: readind of the precepts of the ritual. Above: Silenus musician.

On the left: the Bacchante. Above: bride attire.

THE MODERN TOWN OF POMPEII

Following the eruption of 79 A.D. every trace of the ancient town of Pompeii was lost. Only a vague memory of the town was preserved in the name *Civita* (town) which was given to the countryside that now covered the ancient town. No dwellings were built in the area, which was generically referred to as the "Vallum" or "Valley" and was characterised by an unhealthy climate due to the swamps and marshes.
The modern town of Pompeii, which was originally called "Valle di Pompei" (Valley of Pompeii) was founded in 1875 with a small settlement of 300 people. Today Pompeii has a population of about 25,000 inhabitants.
The history of the modern town is entwined with the work of an extraordinary man called **Bartolo Longo**, a devoutly religious layman who spent his whole life spreading the cult of the Virgin Mary. A lawyer by profession, Bartolo Longo came to the rural district that was to become the town of Pompeii in 1872 as he had been empowered to manage the estate of the **Countess De Fusco**. Faithfully following his inspiration and with the support of the then Bishop of Nola, he started building a church dedicated to **Our Lady of the Rosary**.
The miraculous works achieved by the intercession of the Virgin Mary drew people from near and far while generous financial offerings made it possible to start construction work on the San-

The Sanctuary and its bell-tower by night.

ctuary, which is now a place of pilgrimage.
In 1887 Bartolo Longo dedicated his full attention to the problems of young orphan girls and later, in 1892, to the sons of convicts and finally, in 1922, to their daughters, setting up homes and schools for them.
Bartolo Longo died on 5 October 1926 and was laid to rest in the Chapel that was dedicated to him in 1983. On 7 May 1934 a canonical procedure was initiated for his beatification, which culminated in Rome on 26 October 1980 when **Pope John Paul II** defined him as "the layman who lived his religious commitment to the full".
The monument built in 1962 on the eastern side of the large square that bears Blessed Bartolo Longo's name is dedica-

Image with the Holy Virgin Mary of Pompei.

Inside the Basilica. Central altar.

ted to this devout man.
The bell tower alongside the basilica was built in 1925 and is crowned with a large bronze cross which can be seen from everywhere in the Sarno river valley and serves almost as a lighthouse for all those heading towards Pompeii.
The original church was extended in 1939 to create the modern sanctuary that we can see today.
The main facade was inaugurated on 5 May 1901 after eight years' work under the supervision of the **architect Giovanni Rispoli**. Bartolo Longo intended the church to be a monument to Universal Peace built with the small offerings of people from all over the world.
The inside of the sanctuary is embellished with marble decorations, mosaics and paintings but the central feature is the

Image of Our Lady of the Rosary which thousands of pilgrims come to visit every year.
The painting was restored first in 1875 and subsequently in 1879 before a definitive work of restoration and preservation was carried out in 1965 by the Olivetian Benedictine order in Rome.
The image of the Virgin Mary was crowned by **Pope Paul VI** and then transported to Pompeii in triumph by its faithful followers.
The thousands of ex-voto offerings donated to the Virgin Mary in recognition of the protection received from the Madonna are exhibited in one wing of the Sanctuary.
Here visitors can admire the decorations, precious chalices, corals and cameos, silver statues and numerous paintings describing the various miracles worked.
The large square in the centre of Pompeii was inaugurated in 1887 together with the Via Sacra.
Pompeii officially became a town in its own right on 17 December 1927. The town's economy is predominantly based on tourism and has a number of hotels, restaurants and elegant shops where visitors can while away their time.

Aerial view of the Sanctuary and the bell-tower.

The Mount Vesuvius Museum (Museo Vesuviano)

This small natural history museum is dedicated to its founder **Gian Battista Alfano** and houses an interesting collection of rare minerals gathered during the past eruptions of Mount Vesuvius.
A particularly interesting part of the museum exhibits prints, etchings and photographs of the volcano. The museum is currently housed in the premises belonging to the Works of the Sanctuary and is run by the local Tourist Board. Entry is free of charge.

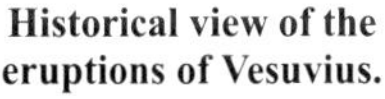

Historical view of the eruptions of Vesuvius.

Plan of the Basilica of the Blessed Virgin of the Rosary

A - Central altar - Throne
B - Entrance to Sacristy
C - Entrance to Crypt

Lateral Altars

1 - St. Vincenzo Ferreri
2 - Sacred Heart of Jesus
3 - St. Thomas D'Aquinas
4 - The Archangel St. Michael
5 - St. Rosa da Lima
6 - St. John the Baptist De La Salle
7 - St. Pius V
8 - St. Catherine of Sienna
9 - St. Joseph
10 - St. Alfonso Maria dei Liguori
11 - St. Francis of Assisi
12 - St. Domenico Guzman

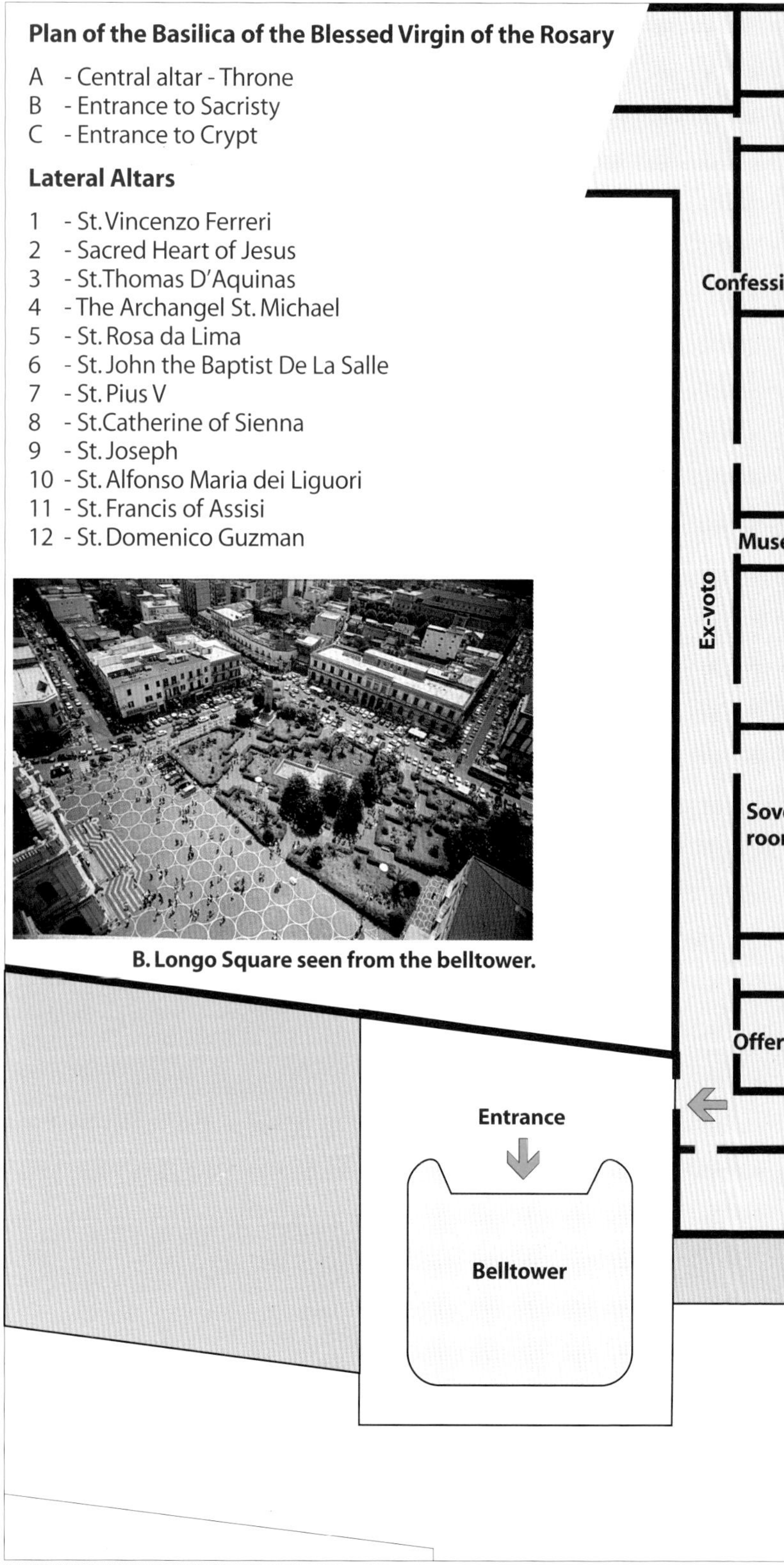

B. Longo Square seen from the belltower.

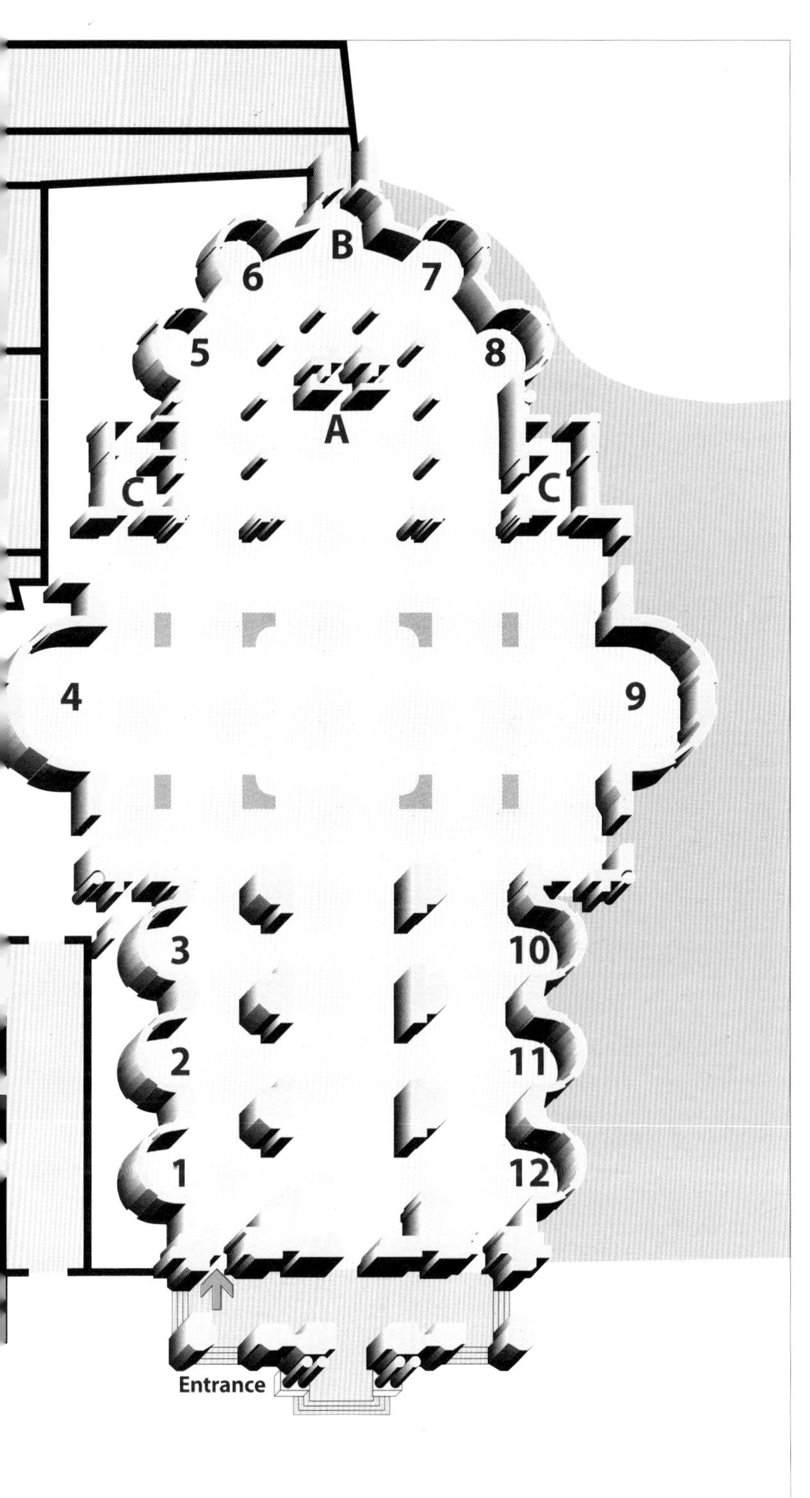
B
6
7
5
8
A
C
C
4
9
3
10
2
11
1
12
Entrance
Bartolo Longo Square

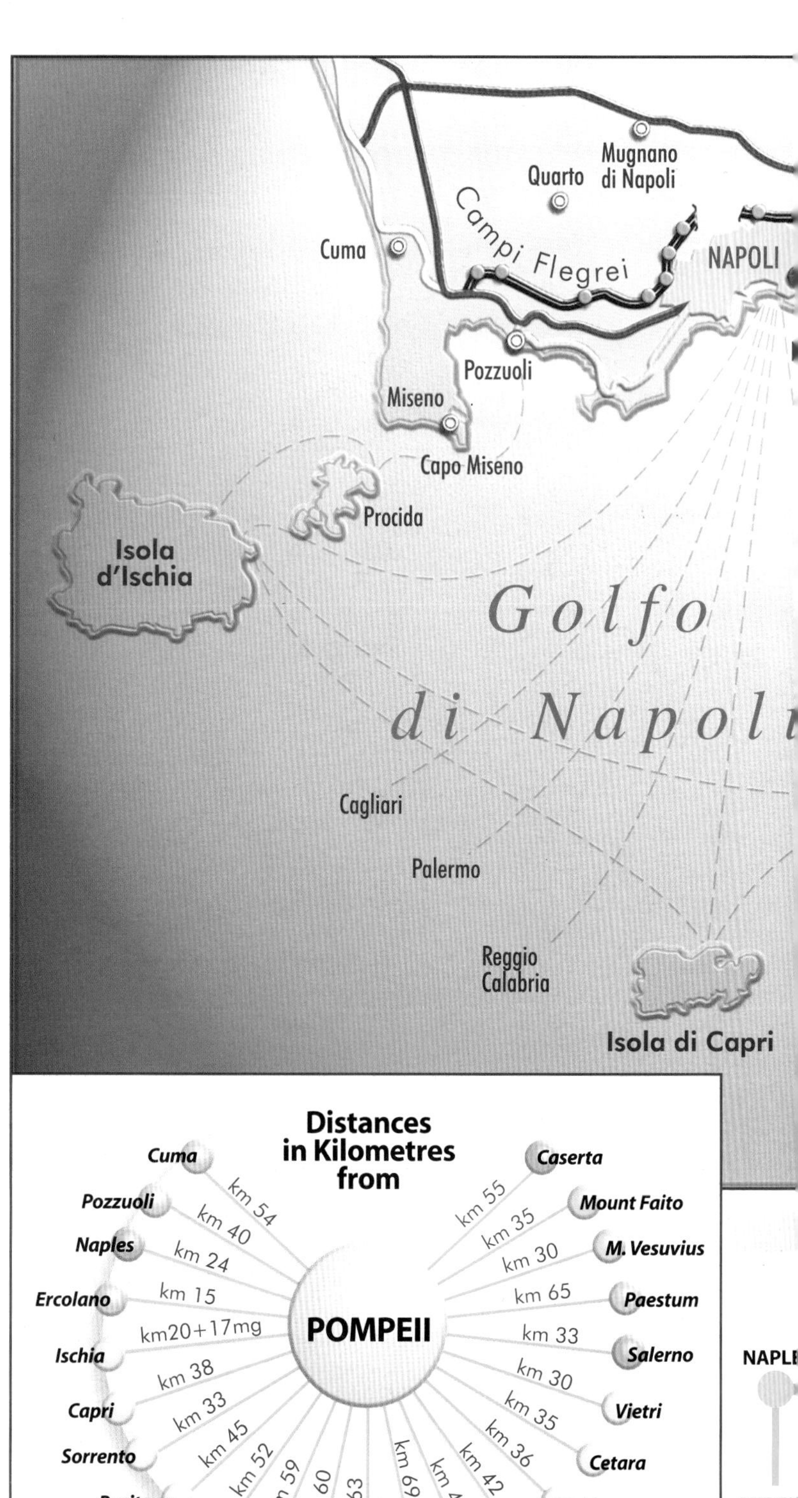
Mugnano
di Napoli
Quarto
Campi Flegrei
Cuma
NAPOLI
Pozzuoli
Miseno
Capo Miseno
Procida
Isola
d'Ischia
Golfo
di Napoli
Cagliari
Palermo
Reggio
Calabria
Isola di Capri
Distances
in Kilometres
from
POMPEII
Cuma
km 54
Pozzuoli
km 40
Naples
km 24
Ercolano
km 15
Ischia
km20+17mg
Capri
km 38
Sorrento
km 33
Positano
km 45
Praiano
km 52
Conca d. Marini
km 59
Amalfi
km 60
Atrani
km 63
Ravello
km 69/36
Minori
km 44
Maiori
km 42
Erchie
km 36
Cetara
km 35
Vietri
km 30
Salerno
km 33
Paestum
km 65
M. Vesuvius
km 30
Mount Faito
km 35
Caserta
km 55

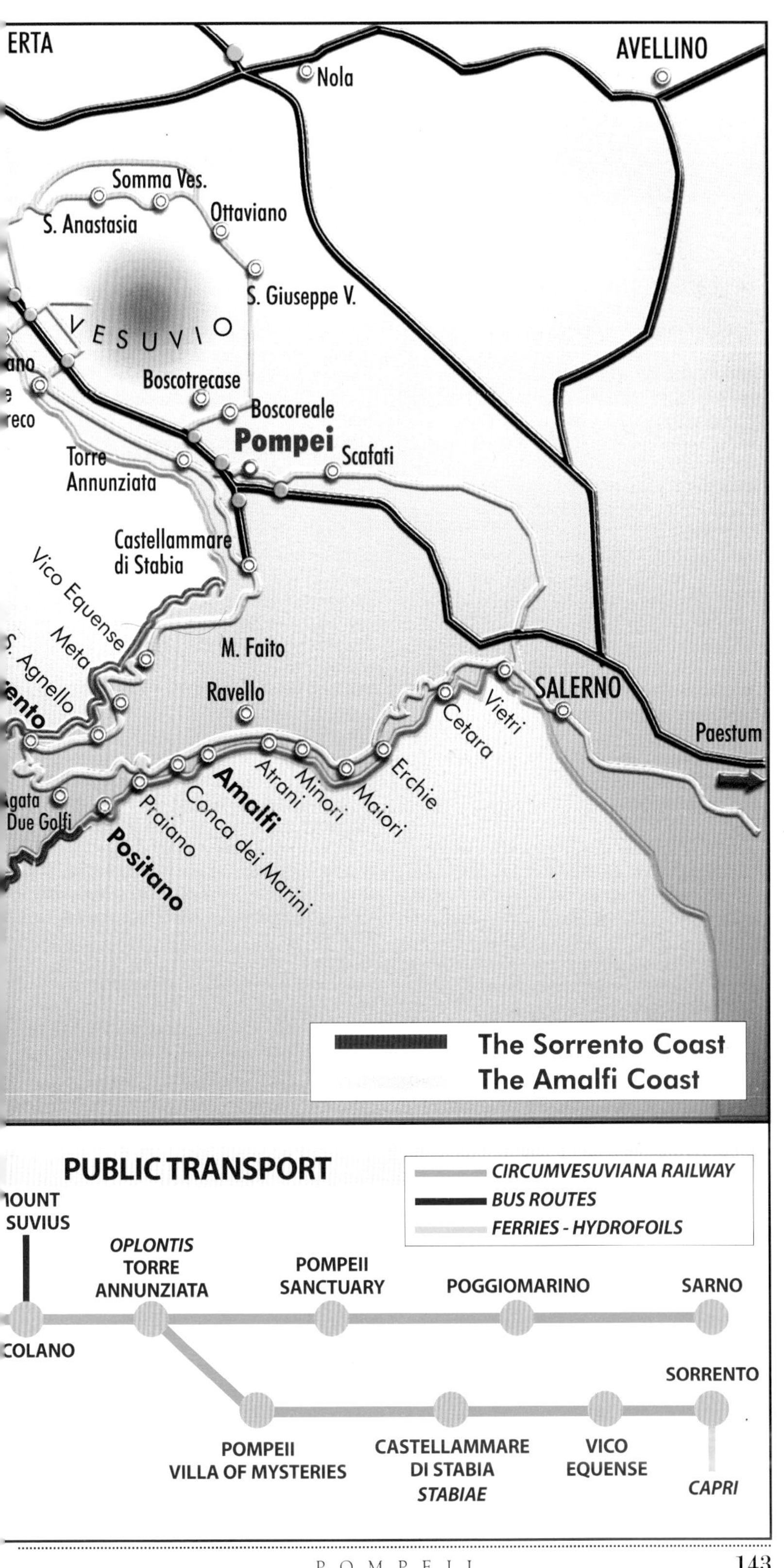
ERTA
Nola
AVELLINO
Somma Ves.
S. Anastasia
Ottaviano
S. Giuseppe V.
VESUVIO
Boscotrecase
Boscoreale
Pompei
Scafati
Torre Annunziata
Castellammare di Stabia
Vico Equense
Meta
S. Agnello
M. Faito
Ravello
SALERNO
Vietri
Cetara
Erchie
Maiori
Minori
Atrani
Amalfi
Conca dei Marini
Praiano
Positano
Due Golfi
Paestum
The Sorrento Coast
The Amalfi Coast
PUBLIC TRANSPORT
CIRCUMVESUVIANA RAILWAY
BUS ROUTES
FERRIES - HYDROFOILS
OPLONTIS
TORRE ANNUNZIATA
POMPEII SANCTUARY
POGGIOMARINO
SARNO
SORRENTO
POMPEII VILLA OF MYSTERIES
CASTELLAMMARE DI STABIA
STABIAE
VICO EQUENSE
CAPRI

Glossary

Amphora. Large terracotta container used predominantly for storing wine.
Apodyterium. Changing room in a Roman baths complex.
Apollo. God of the sun.
Apse. Room or area with a semicircular or polygonal plan.
Atrium. Main room in the house, used for receiving and entertaining guests.
Bacchus. God of wine.
Bucchero or boccaro. Black tinted ceramic work typical of Etruscan production between the 7th and the 5th centuries B.C.
Calidarium. The hottest room in a Roman baths complex where customers could take a hot bath.
Caupona. An inn or tavern.
Cavea. The terraced seating for the public inside Roman theatres.
Centaurs. Mythological figures with a human torso on a horse's body.
Cherub. A winged mythological figure: the offspring of Bacchus and Venus.
Cinnabar. A flame red colour obtained from mercury.
Compluvium. An opening in the ceiling of the atrium to allow light into the house and to collect rain water in a tank on the floor, called the impluvium, of the same size as the compluvium and positioned exactly below it.
Cryptoporticus. A porch or gallery, one or more sides of which are below ground level.
Cubiculum. A bed-chamber, generally small in size.
Decumanus. A main street in a Roman town, running east-west and intersecting with the various cardines which run north-south. This rational street plan was the development of the layout of military camps; in Pompeii the decumanus is Via dell'Abbondanza.
Diaeta. Dining room.
Exedra. A room with seats arranged in a semicircle for relaxation and conversation.
Fresco. A wall painting technique in which the paint is applied directly onto the plaster before it dries.
Frigidarium. A room in a Roman baths complex where customers could take a cold bath.
Hypocaustum. A heating system in which hot air was made to circulate through the cavities deliberately made in walls and floors.
Insula. A housing block formed by the intersection of north-south and east-west streets.
Isis. An Egyptian goddess.
Lanista. Someone who owns, rents or trains gladiators.
Lararium. A small shrine containing the Lares or tutelary gods of the house or district.
Mars. God of war.
Mosaic. A technique for making designs and pictures by juxtaposing small stone blocks or tiles.
Oecus. A room for receptions and celebrations.
Pappamonte. Blackish tufa-stone material obtained from volcanic ashes.
Peristyle. An inner courtyard surrounded by a colonnade with an arcade onto which numerous rooms in the house opened out.
Poppaea. The wife of the Emperor Nero. She owned a superb villa at Oplontis.
Praefurnium. A fire place for heating the Roman baths.
Pumice. Very light and porous stones erupted by the volcano.
Satyrs. Mythological figures from the court of Dionysus.
Sestertius. A Roman coin minted originally in silver but later in bronze.
Sudatorium. A room in a Roman baths complex similar to a modern-day sauna.
Suspensurae. Small brick columns supporting a floor. They were used to create a cavity beneath the floor for heating purposes (see Hypocaustum).
Taberna. A shop.
Tablinum. A room in a Roman house between the atrium and the peristyle which was used as a sort of office for the household business. This was where the tabulae, or accounts and other documents, were kept.
Tepidarium. A room in a Roman baths complex where customers could take a warm bath.
Tetrastyle. A building, room or area with four columns.
Thermopolium. Restaurant-inn.
These had no real kitchen up until the 1st century B.C. as certain regulations regarding law and order tried to restrict sales to just wine.
Titus. The Emperor reigning at the time of the eruption. He succeeded his father Titus Flavius Vespasianus.
Triclinium. Dining room where members of the household and guests could eat a meal reclining on couches.
Venationes. Shows involving armed combat or wild animal hunts, held in the Amphitheatre.
Vestibulum. An entrance hall.